# the poetry
### of
# Walt
# Whitman

9781788287777

# the poetry of Walt Whitman

This edition published in 2019 by Arcturus Publishing Limited
26/27 Bickels Yard, 151–153 Bermondsey Street,
London SE1 3HA

AD006342US

Printed in the UK

# Contents

# Introduction

Walt Whitman, the "bard of democracy," is regarded as one of America's greatest poets. Largely ignored during his lifetime, few poets have left such a legacy. Inspired by the possibilities he saw in democracy, his poems were provocative, awkward, and radical, earning him criticism from conservative quarters. In turn, however, they inspired the Surrealists, the artists of the New York School and the Beat Poets among others. Today, his name lives on in schools, shopping malls and bridges, his words are used by Levi's and Apple to sell jeans and iPads and his reputation used as a plot device for the TV show *Breaking Bad*.

Born into a large, working-class family in West Hills, Long Island, on May 31, 1819, Walt Whitman began his life alongside that of a new nation. The newly formed United States (George Washington had only taken office 30 years earlier) was in a ferment of development. He had a curious mind, working as an office boy, an apprentice in the printing trade, and as a teacher. He pursued his literary interests, dabbling in poetry, short stories, and a novel, before deciding to be a journalist. He proved to be a volatile journalist with sharp opinions and a sharper wit, championing the working man and often expressing radical opinions on social, economic, and political reform in local and national issues.

In 1848, Whitman visited New Orleans. The city made a significant impression on him. He loved its multi-cultures and mixtures of language and cuisine, which enabled him to see the possibilities of a distinctive Americanism emerging from the melting pot of race and culture. But he was horrified by the slave auctions in Lafayette Square and never forgot seeing humans on the selling blocks, an experience he would later use in his poem "I Sing the Body Electric.".

It is difficult to understand the transformation that took

place in Whitman's poetry during the late 1840s, which saw him abandon traditional styles, meter, and language, replacing them with a unique style of free verse with prosaic rhythms, Old Testament repetition, and loud, earthy language. At the same time, his politics, in particular his views on the slave trade—an issue that was dividing the nation—were changing. New friendships with the radical thinkers of the day freed his thinking from its traditional constraints.

The first iterations of this new style came in a slim volume entitled *Leaves of Grass*, published in 1855, containing 12 untitled poems. The first poem, later rewritten and titled "Song of Myself," sets out his stall, stating that everything and everyone— good and bad, male and female, free and not—is equal. In the preface, he wrote, "The United States themselves are essentially the greatest poem." It seems that he had found the right voice to match his great subject: the unity and diversity of the American self, in this case embodied by the all-powerful "I" through which he speaks to the reader.

It attracted little attention at first, though his fellow poet Ralph Waldo Emerson (1803–82) wrote to Whitman to praise the collection as "the most extraordinary piece of wit and wisdom" to come from an American pen. The following year saw a revised edition, which contained 32 poems including "Sun-Down Poem" (later renamed "Crossing Brooklyn Ferry"). A third edition followed in 1860 and attracted more attention, particularly because of a series of poems exploring male–female eroticism. But the Civil War, which began the following year, caused the publisher to go bankrupt.

In 1862, Whitman traveled to Fredericksburg in search of his brother George who had been wounded while fighting for the Union. What he saw on the battlefield inspired his poetic nature. In 1865, came a new publication called *Drum-Taps*. The solemn nature of poems such as "Beat! Beat! Drums!" and "Vigil

Strange I Kept on the Field One Night" helped readers understand what war was really like. A second edition followed, which included his elegy on Abraham Lincoln, "When Lilacs Last in the Dooryard Bloom'd."

Over the next two decades, Whitman continued to tinker with *Leaves of Grass*, endlessly editing the existing poems and adding new material. The last edition—published shortly before his death in 1892—contained a hefty 400 poems. In retrospect, it might seem that his aim all along had been to gather his work together in one sustained epic. Perhaps it is this epic quality that appeals so strongly today, embodying as it does the nature and scale of the American continent, character, and nature; linking black to white, master to slave, and the self to the state. Whitman's work has become the embodiment of the American self, the American "I," reminding readers, even today, of democracy's continuing potential.

This collection, which includes all his major works, illustrates the astonishing originality and intensity of Whitman's work, covering race, politics, sexual emancipation, and what it means to be an American.

# The Mississippi At Midnight

How solemn! sweeping this dense black tide!
    No friendly lights i' the heaven o'er us;
A murky darkness on either side,
    And kindred darkness all before us!

Now, drawn nearer, the shelving rim,
    Weird-like shadows suddenly rise;
Shapes of mist and phantoms dim
    Baffle the gazer's straining eyes.

River fiends, with malignant faces!
    Wild and wide their arms are thrown,
As if to clutch in fatal embraces
    Him who sails their realms upon.

Then, by the trick of our swift motion,
    Straight, tall giants, an army vast,
Rank by rank, like the waves of ocean,
    On the shore march stiffly past,

How solemn! the river a trailing pall,
    Which takes, but never again gives back;
And moonless and starless the heaven's arch'd wall,
    Responding an equal black!

Oh, tireless waters! like Life's quick dream,
    Onward and onward ever hurrying—
Like Death in this midnight hour you seem,
    Life in your chill drops greedily burying!

## A Boston Ballad

To get betimes in Boston town I rose this morning early,
Here's a good place at the corner, I must stand and see the
show.

Clear the way there Jonathan!
Way for the President's marshal—way for the government
cannon!
Way for the Federal foot and dragoons, (and the apparitions
copiously tumbling.)

I love to look on the Stars and Stripes, I hope the fifes will
play Yankee Doodle.

How bright shine the cutlasses of the foremost troops!
Every man holds his revolver, marching stiff through Boston
town.

A fog follows, antiques of the same come limping,
Some appear wooden-legged, and some appear bandaged
and bloodless.

Why this is indeed a show—it has called the dead out of
the earth!
The old graveyards of the hills have hurried to see!
Phantoms! phantoms countless by flank and rear!
Cock'd hats of mothy mould—crutches made of mist!
Arms in slings—old men leaning on young men's shoulders.

What troubles you Yankee phantoms? what is all this chat-
tering of bare gums?

Does the ague convulse your limbs? do you mistake your
  crutches for firelocks and level them?

If you blind your eyes with tears you will not see the
  President's marshal,
If you groan such groans you might balk the government
  cannon.

For shame old maniacs—bring down those toss'd arms, and
  let your white hair be,
Here gape your great grandsons, their wives gaze at them
  from the windows,
See how well dress'd, see how orderly they conduct themselves.

Worse and worse—can't you stand it? are you retreating?
Is this hour with the living too dead for you?

Retreat then—pell-mell!
To your graves—back—back to the hills old limpers!
I do not think you belong here anyhow.

But there is one thing that belongs here—shall I tell you
  what it is, gentlemen of Boston?

I will whisper it to the Mayor, he shall send a committee
  to England,
They shall get a grant from the Parliament, go with a cart
  to the royal vault,
Dig out King George's coffin, unwrap him quick from the
  grave-clothes, box up his bones for a journey,

Find a swift Yankee clipper—here is freight for you, black-
bellied clipper,
Up with your anchor—shake out your sails—steer straight
toward Boston bay.

Now call for the President's marshal again, bring out the
government cannon,
Fetch home the roarers from Congress, make another
procession,
guard it with foot and dragoons.

This centre-piece for them;
Look, all orderly citizens—look from the windows, women!

The committee open the box, set up the regal ribs, glue
those that will not stay,
Clap the skull on top of the ribs, and clap a crown on top
of the skull.

You have got your revenge, old buster—the crown is come
to its own, and more than its own.

Stick your hands in your pockets, Jonathan—you are a made
man from this day,
You are mighty cute—and here is one of your bargains.

# Song of Myself

**1**

I celebrate myself, and sing myself,
And what I assume you shall assume,
For every atom belonging to me as good belongs to you.

I loafe and invite my soul,
I lean and loafe at my ease observing a spear of summer
grass.

My tongue, every atom of my blood, form'd from this soil,
this air,
Born here of parents born here from parents the same, and
their parents the same,
I, now thirty-seven years old in perfect health begin,
Hoping to cease not till death.

Creeds and schools in abeyance,
Retiring back a while sufficed at what they are, but never
forgotten,
I harbor for good or bad, I permit to speak at every hazard,
Nature without check with original energy.

**2**

Houses and rooms are full of perfumes, the shelves are
crowded with perfumes,
I breathe the fragrance myself and know it and like it,
The distillation would intoxicate me also, but I shall not let
it.

The atmosphere is not a perfume, it has no taste of the
distillation, it is odorless,
It is for my mouth forever, I am in love with it,
I will go to the bank by the wood and become undisguised
and naked,
I am mad for it to be in contact with me.

The smoke of my own breath,
Echoes, ripples, buzz'd whispers, love-root, silk-thread,
crotch and vine,
My respiration and inspiration, the beating of my heart, the
passing of blood and air through my lungs,
The sniff of green leaves and dry leaves, and of the shore
and dark-color'd sea-rocks, and of hay in the barn,
The sound of the belch'd words of my voice loos'd to the
eddies of the wind,
A few light kisses, a few embraces, a reaching around of
arms,
The play of shine and shade on the trees as the supple boughs
wag,
The delight alone or in the rush of the streets, or along the
fields and hill-sides,
The feeling of health, the full-noon trill, the song of me
rising from bed and meeting the sun.

Have you reckon'd a thousand acres much? have you reckon'd
the earth much?
Have you practis'd so long to learn to read?
Have you felt so proud to get at the meaning of poems?

Stop this day and night with me and you shall possess the
origin of all poems,

You shall possess the good of the earth and sun, (there are millions of suns left,)
You shall no longer take things at second or third hand, nor look through the eyes of the dead, nor feed on the spectres in books,
You shall not look through my eyes either, nor take things from me,
You shall listen to all sides and filter them from your self.

### 3

I have heard what the talkers were talking, the talk of the beginning and the end,
But I do not talk of the beginning or the end.

There was never any more inception than there is now,
Nor any more youth or age than there is now,
And will never be any more perfection than there is now,
Nor any more heaven or hell than there is now.

Urge and urge and urge,
Always the procreant urge of the world.

Out of the dimness opposite equals advance, always substance and increase, always sex,
Always a knit of identity, always distinction, always a breed of life.

To elaborate is no avail, learn'd and unlearn'd feel that it is so.

Sure as the most certain sure, plumb in the uprights, well entretied, braced in the beams,

Stout as a horse, affectionate, haughty, electrical,
I and this mystery here we stand.

Clear and sweet is my soul, and clear and sweet is all that
is not my soul.

Lack one lacks both, and the unseen is proved by the seen,
Till that becomes unseen and receives proof in its turn.

Showing the best and dividing it from the worst age vexes
age,
Knowing the perfect fitness and equanimity of things, while
they discuss I am silent, and go bathe and admire myself.

Welcome is every organ and attribute of me, and of any
man hearty and clean,
Not an inch nor a particle of an inch is vile, and none shall
be less familiar than the rest.

I am satisfied—I see, dance, laugh, sing;
As the hugging and loving bed-fellow sleeps at my side
through the night, and withdraws at the peep of the day
with stealthy tread,
Leaving me baskets cover'd with white towels swelling the
house with their plenty,
Shall I postpone my acceptation and realization and scream
at my eyes,
That they turn from gazing after and down the road,
And forthwith cipher and show me to a cent,
Exactly the value of one and exactly the value of two, and
which is ahead?

**4**

Trippers and askers surround me,
People I meet, the effect upon me of my early life or the
    ward and city I live in, or the nation,
The latest dates, discoveries, inventions, societies, authors
    old and new,
My dinner, dress, associates, looks, compliments, dues,
The real or fancied indifference of some man or woman I
    love,
The sickness of one of my folks or of myself, or ill-doing
    or loss or lack of money, or depressions or exaltations,
Battles, the horrors of fratricidal war, the fever of doubtful
    news, the fitful events;
These come to me days and nights and go from me again,
But they are not the Me myself.
Apart from the pulling and hauling stands what I am,
Stands amused, complacent, compassionating, idle, unitary,
Looks down, is erect, or bends an arm on an impalpable
    certain rest,
Looking with side-curved head curious what will come next,
Both in and out of the game and watching and wondering
    at it.
Backward I see in my own days where I sweated through
    fog with linguists and contenders,
I have no mockings or arguments, I witness and wait.

**5**

I believe in you my soul, the other I am must not abase
    itself to you,
And you must not be abased to the other.

Loafe with me on the grass, loose the stop from your throat,

Not words, not music or rhyme I want, not custom or
    lecture, not even the best,
Only the lull I like, the hum of your valved voice.


I mind how once we lay such a transparent summer morning,
How you settled your head athwart my hips and gently
    turn'd over upon me,
And parted the shirt from my bosom-bone, and plunged
    your tongue to my bare-stript heart,
And reach'd till you felt my beard, and reach'd till you held
    my feet.


Swiftly arose and spread around me the peace and knowledge
    that pass all the argument of the earth,
And I know that the hand of God is the promise of my own,
And I know that the spirit of God is the brother of my own,
And that all the men ever born are also my brothers, and
    the women my sisters and lovers,
And that a kelson of the creation is love,
And limitless are leaves stiff or drooping in the fields,
And brown ants in the little wells beneath them,
And mossy scabs of the worm fence, heap'd stones, elder,
    mullein and poke-weed.


**6**

A child said *What is the grass?* fetching it to me with full hands;
How could I answer the child? I do not know what it is any
    more than he.


I guess it must be the flag of my disposition, out of hopeful
    green stuff woven.

Or I guess it is the handkerchief of the Lord,
A scented gift and remembrancer designedly dropt,
Bearing the owner's name someway in the corners, that we
   may see and remark, and say *Whose?*

Or I guess the grass is itself a child, the produced babe of
   the vegetation.

Or I guess it is a uniform hieroglyphic,
And it means, Sprouting alike in broad zones and narrow
   zones,
Growing among black folks as among white,
Kanuck, Tuckahoe, Congressman, Cuff, I give them the same,
   I receive them the same.

And now it seems to me the beautiful uncut hair of graves.

Tenderly will I use you curling grass,
It may be you transpire from the breasts of young men,
It may be if I had known them I would have loved them,
It may be you are from old people, or from offspring taken
   soon out of their mothers' laps,
And here you are the mothers' laps.

This grass is very dark to be from the white heads of old
   mothers,
Darker than the colorless beards of old men,
Dark to come from under the faint red roofs of mouths.

O I perceive after all so many uttering tongues,
And I perceive they do not come from the roofs of mouths
   for nothing.

I wish I could translate the hints about the dead young men
    and women,
And the hints about old men and mothers, and the offspring
    taken soon out of their laps.

What do you think has become of the young and old men?
And what do you think has become of the women and
    children?

They are alive and well somewhere,
The smallest sprout shows there is really no death,
And if ever there was it led forward life, and does not wait
    at the end to arrest it,
And ceas'd the moment life appear'd.

All goes onward and outward, nothing collapses,
And to die is different from what any one supposed, and
    luckier.

### 7

Has any one supposed it lucky to be born?
I hasten to inform him or her it is just as lucky to die, and
    I know it.

I pass death with the dying and birth with the new-wash'd
    babe, and am not contain'd between my hat and boots,
And peruse manifold objects, no two alike and every one
    good,
The earth good and the stars good, and their adjuncts all good.

I am not an earth nor an adjunct of an earth,
I am the mate and companion of people, all just as immortal
   and fathomless as myself,
(They do not know how immortal, but I know.)

Every kind for itself and its own, for me mine male and
   female,
For me those that have been boys and that love women,
For me the man that is proud and feels how it stings to be
   slighted,
For me the sweet-heart and the old maid, for me mothers
   and the mothers of mothers,
For me lips that have smiled, eyes that have shed tears,
For me children and the begetters of children.

Undrape! you are not guilty to me, nor stale nor discarded,
I see through the broadcloth and gingham whether or no,
And am around, tenacious, acquisitive, tireless, and cannot
   be shaken away.

## 8
The little one sleeps in its cradle,
I lift the gauze and look a long time, and silently brush away
   flies with my hand.

The youngster and the red-faced girl turn aside up the bushy
   hill,
I peeringly view them from the top.

The suicide sprawls on the bloody floor of the bedroom,
I witness the corpse with its dabbled hair, I note where the
   pistol has fallen.

The blab of the pave, tires of carts, sluff of boot-soles, talk
of the promenaders,
The heavy omnibus, the driver with his interrogating thumb,
the clank of the shod horses on the granite floor,
The snow-sleighs, clinking, shouted jokes, pelts of snow-balls,
The hurrahs for popular favorites, the fury of rous'd mobs,
The flap of the curtain'd litter, a sick man inside borne to
the hospital,
The meeting of enemies, the sudden oath, the blows and fall,
The excited crowd, the policeman with his star quickly
working his passage to the centre of the crowd,
The impassive stones that receive and return so many echoes,
What groans of over-fed or half-starv'd who fall sunstruck
or in fits,
What exclamations of women taken suddenly who hurry
home and give birth to babes,
What living and buried speech is always vibrating here, what
howls restrain'd by decorum,
Arrests of criminals, slights, adulterous offers made, accept-
ances, rejections with convex lips,
I mind them or the show or resonance of them—I come
and I depart.


9
The big doors of the country barn stand open and ready,
The dried grass of the harvest-time loads the slow-drawn
wagon,
The clear light plays on the brown gray and green intertinged,
The armfuls are pack'd to the sagging mow.

I am there, I help, I came stretch'd atop of the load,
I felt its soft jolts, one leg reclined on the other,

I jump from the cross-beams and seize the clover and timothy,
And roll head over heels and tangle my hair full of wisps.


**10**

Alone far in the wilds and mountains I hunt,
Wandering amazed at my own lightness and glee,
In the late afternoon choosing a safe spot to pass the night,
Kindling a fire and broiling the fresh-kill'd game,
Falling asleep on the gather'd leaves with my dog and gun
   by my side.


The Yankee clipper is under her sky-sails, she cuts the sparkle
   and scud,
My eyes settle the land, I bend at her prow or shout joyously
   from the deck.


The boatmen and clam-diggers arose early and stopt
   for me,
I tuck'd my trowser-ends in my boots and went and had a
   good time;
You should have been with us that day round the chowder-
   kettle.


I saw the marriage of the trapper in the open air in the far
   west, the bride was a red girl,
Her father and his friends sat near cross-legged and dumbly
   smoking, they had moccasins to their feet and large thick
   blankets hanging from their shoulders,
On a bank lounged the trapper, he was drest mostly in skins,
   his luxuriant beard and curls protected his neck, he held
   his bride by the hand,
She had long eyelashes, her head was bare, her coarse straight

locks descended upon her voluptuous limbs and reach'd to her feet.

The runaway slave came to my house and stopt outside,
I heard his motions crackling the twigs of the woodpile,
Through the swung half-door of the kitchen I saw him limpsy and weak,
And went where he sat on a log and led him in and assured him,
And brought water and fill'd a tub for his sweated body and bruis'd feet,
And gave him a room that enter'd from my own, and gave him some coarse clean clothes,
And remember perfectly well his revolving eyes and his awkwardness,
And remember putting plasters on the galls of his neck and ankles;
He staid with me a week before he was recuperated and pass'd north,
I had him sit next me at table, my fire-lock lean'd in the corner.

## 11

Twenty-eight young men bathe by the shore,
Twenty-eight young men and all so friendly;
Twenty-eight years of womanly life and all so lonesome.

She owns the fine house by the rise of the bank,
She hides handsome and richly drest aft the blinds of the window.

Which of the young men does she like the best?

Ah the homeliest of them is beautiful to her.

Where are you off to, lady? for I see you,
You splash in the water there, yet stay stock still in your room.

Dancing and laughing along the beach came the twenty-ninth
    bather,
The rest did not see her, but she saw them and loved them.

The beards of the young men glisten'd with wet, it ran from
    their long hair,
Little streams pass'd all over their bodies.

An unseen hand also pass'd over their bodies,
It descended tremblingly from their temples and ribs.

The young men float on their backs, their white bellies bulge
    to the sun, they do not ask who seizes fast to them,
They do not know who puffs and declines with pendant
    and bending arch,
They do not think whom they souse with spray.

## 12

The butcher-boy puts off his killing-clothes, or sharpens his
    knife at the stall in the market,
I loiter enjoying his repartee and his shuffle and break-down.

Blacksmiths with grimed and hairy chests environ the anvil,
Each has his main-sledge, they are all out, there is a great
    heat in the fire.

From the cinder-strew'd threshold I follow their movements,

The lithe sheer of their waists plays even with their massive
   arms,
Overhand the hammers swing, overhand so slow, overhand
   so sure,
They do not hasten, each man hits in his place.

**13**

The negro holds firmly the reins of his four horses, the
   block swags underneath on its tied-over chain,
The negro that drives the long dray of the stone-yard, steady
   and tall he stands pois'd on one leg on the string-piece,
His blue shirt exposes his ample neck and breast and loosens
   over his hip-band,
His glance is calm and commanding, he tosses the slouch
   of his hat away from his forehead,
The sun falls on his crispy hair and mustache, falls on the
   black of his polish'd and perfect limbs.

I behold the picturesque giant and love him, and I do not
   stop there,
I go with the team also.

In me the caresser of life wherever moving, backward as
   well as forward sluing,
To niches aside and junior bending, not a person or object
   missing,
Absorbing all to myself and for this song.

Oxen that rattle the yoke and chain or halt in the leafy shade,
   what is that you express in your eyes?
It seems to me more than all the print I have read in my life.

My tread scares the wood-drake and wood-duck on my
　　distant and day-long ramble,
They rise together, they slowly circle around.

I believe in those wing'd purposes,
And acknowledge red, yellow, white, playing within me,
And consider green and violet and the tufted crown inten-
　　tional,
And do not call the tortoise unworthy because she is not
　　something else,
And the jay in the woods never studied the gamut, yet trills
　　pretty well to me,
And the look of the bay mare shames silliness out of me.

**14**
The wild gander leads his flock through the cool night,
Ya-honk he says, and sounds it down to me like an invitation,
The pert may suppose it meaningless, but I listening close,
Find its purpose and place up there toward the wintry sky.

The sharp-hoof'd moose of the north, the cat on the house-
　　sill, the chickadee, the prairie-dog,
The litter of the grunting sow as they tug at her teats,
The brood of the turkey-hen and she with her half-spread
　　wings,
I see in them and myself the same old law.

The press of my foot to the earth springs a hundred affections,
They scorn the best I can do to relate them.

I am enamour'd of growing out-doors,
Of men that live among cattle or taste of the ocean or woods,

Of the builders and steerers of ships and the wielders of
    axes and mauls, and the drivers of horses,
I can eat and sleep with them week in and week out.

What is commonest, cheapest, nearest, easiest, is Me,
Me going in for my chances, spending for vast returns,
Adorning myself to bestow myself on the first that will take
    me,
Not asking the sky to come down to my good will,
Scattering it freely forever.

## 15

The pure contralto sings in the organ loft,
The carpenter dresses his plank, the tongue of his foreplane
    whistles its wild ascending lisp,
The married and unmarried children ride home to their
    Thanksgiving dinner,
The pilot seizes the king-pin, he heaves down with a strong
    arm,
The mate stands braced in the whale-boat, lance and harpoon
    are ready,
The duck-shooter walks by silent and cautious stretches,
The deacons are ordain'd with cross'd hands at the altar,
The spinning-girl retreats and advances to the hum of the
    big wheel,
The farmer stops by the bars as he walks on a First-day loafe
    and looks at the oats and rye,
The lunatic is carried at last to the asylum a confirm'd case,
(He will never sleep any more as he did in the cot in his
    mother's bed-room;)
The jour printer with gray head and gaunt jaws works at
    his case,

He turns his quid of tobacco while his eyes blurr with the
  manuscript;
The malform'd limbs are tied to the surgeon's table,
What is removed drops horribly in a pail;
The quadroon girl is sold at the auction-stand, the drunkard
  nods by the bar-room stove,
The machinist rolls up his sleeves, the policeman travels his
  beat, the gate-keeper marks who pass,
The young fellow drives the express-wagon, (I love him,
  though I do not know him;)
The half-breed straps on his light boots to compete in the
  race,
The western turkey-shooting draws old and young, some
  lean on their rifles, some sit on logs,
Out from the crowd steps the marksman, takes his position,
  levels his piece;
The groups of newly-come immigrants cover the wharf or
  levee,
As the woolly-pates hoe in the sugar-field, the overseer views
  them from his saddle,
The bugle calls in the ball-room, the gentlemen run for their
  partners, the dancers bow to each other,
The youth lies awake in the cedar-roof'd garret and harks
  to the musical rain,
The Wolverine sets traps on the creek that helps fill the Huron,
The squaw wrapt in her yellow-hemm'd cloth is offering
  moccasins and bead-bags for sale,
The connoisseur peers along the exhibition-gallery with
  half-shut eyes bent sideways,
As the deck-hands make fast the steamboat the plank is
  thrown for the shore-going passengers,
The young sister holds out the skein while the elder sister

winds it off in a ball, and stops now and then for the knots,

The one-year wife is recovering and happy having a week ago borne her first child,

The clean-hair'd Yankee girl works with her sewing-machine or in the factory or mill,

The paving-man leans on his two-handed rammer, the reporter's lead flies swiftly over the note-book, the sign-painter is lettering with blue and gold,

The canal boy trots on the tow-path, the book-keeper counts at his desk, the shoemaker waxes his thread,

The conductor beats time for the band and all the performers follow him,

The child is baptized, the convert is making his first professions,

The regatta is spread on the bay, the race is begun, (how the white sails sparkle!)

The drover watching his drove sings out to them that would stray,

The pedler sweats with his pack on his back, (the purchaser higgling about the odd cent;)

The bride unrumples her white dress, the minute-hand of the clock moves slowly,

The opium-eater reclines with rigid head and just-open'd lips,

The prostitute draggles her shawl, her bonnet bobs on her tipsy and pimpled neck,

The crowd laugh at her blackguard oaths, the men jeer and wink to each other,

(Miserable! I do not laugh at your oaths nor jeer you;)

The President holding a cabinet council is surrounded by the great Secretaries,

On the piazza walk three matrons stately and friendly with twined arms,

The crew of the fish-smack pack repeated layers of halibut in the hold,

The Missourian crosses the plains toting his wares and his cattle,

As the fare-collector goes through the train he gives notice by the jingling of loose change,

The floor-men are laying the floor, the tinners are tinning the roof, the masons are calling for mortar,

In single file each shouldering his hod pass onward the laborers;

Seasons pursuing each other the indescribable crowd is gather'd, it is the fourth of Seventh-month, (what salutes of cannon and small arms!)

Seasons pursuing each other the plougher ploughs, the mower mows, and the winter-grain falls in the ground;

Off on the lakes the pike-fisher watches and waits by the hole in the frozen surface,

The stumps stand thick round the clearing, the squatter strikes deep with his axe,

Flatboatmen make fast towards dusk near the cotton-wood or pecan-trees,

Coon-seekers go through the regions of the Red river or through those drain'd by the Tennessee, or through those of the Arkansas,

Torches shine in the dark that hangs on the Chattahooche or Altamahaw,

Patriarchs sit at supper with sons and grandsons and great-grandsons around them,

In walls of adobie, in canvas tents, rest hunters and trappers after their day's sport,

The city sleeps and the country sleeps,

The living sleep for their time, the dead sleep for their
time,
The old husband sleeps by his wife and the young husband
sleeps by his wife;
And these tend inward to me, and I tend outward to them,
And such as it is to be of these more or less I am,
And of these one and all I weave the song of myself.

## 16

I am of old and young, of the foolish as much as the wise,
Regardless of others, ever regardful of others,
Maternal as well as paternal, a child as well as a man,
Stuff'd with the stuff that is coarse and stuff'd with the stuff
that is fine,
One of the Nation of many nations, the smallest the same
and the largest the same,
A Southerner soon as a Northerner, a planter nonchalant
and hospitable down by the Oconee I live,
A Yankee bound my own way ready for trade, my joints the
limberest joints on earth and the sternest joints on earth,
A Kentuckian walking the vale of the Elkhorn in my deer-
skin leggings, a Louisianian or Georgian,
A boatman over lakes or bays or along coasts, a Hoosier,
Badger, Buckeye;
At home on Kanadian snow-shoes or up in the bush, or
with fishermen off Newfoundland,
At home in the fleet of ice-boats, sailing with the rest and
tacking,
At home on the hills of Vermont or in the woods of Maine,
or the Texan ranch,
Comrade of Californians, comrade of free North-Westerners,
(loving their big proportions,)

Comrade of raftsmen and coalmen, comrade of all who
    shake hands and welcome to drink and meat,
A learner with the simplest, a teacher of the thoughtfullest,
A novice beginning yet experient of myriads of seasons,
Of every hue and caste am I, of every rank and religion,
A farmer, mechanic, artist, gentleman, sailor, quaker,
Prisoner, fancy-man, rowdy, lawyer, physician, priest.

I resist any thing better than my own diversity,
Breathe the air but leave plenty after me,
And am not stuck up, and am in my place.

(The moth and the fish-eggs are in their place,
The bright suns I see and the dark suns I cannot see are in
    their place,
The palpable is in its place and the impalpable is in its place.)

## 17

These are really the thoughts of all men in all ages and lands,
    they are not original with me,
If they are not yours as much as mine they are nothing, or
    next to nothing,
If they are not the riddle and the untying of the riddle they
    are nothing,
If they are not just as close as they are distant they are nothing.

This is the grass that grows wherever the land is and the
    water is,
This the common air that bathes the globe.

## 18

With music strong I come, with my cornets and my drums,

I play not marches for accepted victors only, I play marches
   for conquer'd and slain persons.

Have you heard that it was good to gain the day?
I also say it is good to fall, battles are lost in the same spirit
   in which they are won.

I beat and pound for the dead,
I blow through my embouchures my loudest and gayest for
   them.

Vivas to those who have fail'd!
And to those whose war-vessels sank in the sea!
And to those themselves who sank in the sea!
And to all generals that lost engagements, and all overcome
   heroes!
And the numberless unknown heroes equal to the greatest
   heroes known!

**19**

This is the meal equally set, this the meat for natural hunger,
It is for the wicked just same as the righteous, I make
   appointments with all,
I will not have a single person slighted or left away,
The kept-woman, sponger, thief, are hereby invited,
The heavy-lipp'd slave is invited, the venerealee is invited;
There shall be no difference between them and the rest.

This is the press of a bashful hand, this the float and odor
   of hair,
This the touch of my lips to yours, this the murmur of yearning,
This the far-off depth and height reflecting my own face,

This the thoughtful merge of myself, and the outlet again.

Do you guess I have some intricate purpose?
Well I have, for the Fourth-month showers have, and the
   mica on the side of a rock has.

Do you take it I would astonish?
Does the daylight astonish? does the early redstart twittering
   through the woods?
Do I astonish more than they?

This hour I tell things in confidence,
I might not tell everybody, but I will tell you.

**20**
Who goes there? hankering, gross, mystical, nude;
How is it I extract strength from the beef I eat?

What is a man anyhow? what am I? what are you?

All I mark as my own you shall offset it with your own,
Else it were time lost listening to me.

I do not snivel that snivel the world over,
That months are vacuums and the ground but wallow and
   filth.

Whimpering and truckling fold with powders for invalids,
   conformity goes to the fourth-remov'd,
I wear my hat as I please indoors or out.

Why should I pray? why should I venerate and be ceremonious?

Having pried through the strata, analyzed to a hair, counsel'd
  with doctors and calculated close,
I find no sweeter fat than sticks to my own bones.

In all people I see myself, none more and not one a barley-
  corn less,
And the good or bad I say of myself I say of them.

I know I am solid and sound,
To me the converging objects of the universe perpetually flow,
All are written to me, and I must get what the writing means.

I know I am deathless,
I know this orbit of mine cannot be swept by a carpenter's
  compass,
I know I shall not pass like a child's carlacue cut with a
  burnt stick at night.

I know I am august,
I do not trouble my spirit to vindicate itself or be understood,
I see that the elementary laws never apologize,
(I reckon I behave no prouder than the level I plant my
  house by, after all.)

I exist as I am, that is enough,
If no other in the world be aware I sit content,
And if each and all be aware I sit content.

One world is aware and by far the largest to me, and that
  is myself,
And whether I come to my own to-day or in ten thousand
  or ten million years,

I can cheerfully take it now, or with equal cheerfulness I
   can wait.

My foothold is tenon'd and mortis'd in granite,
I laugh at what you call dissolution,
And I know the amplitude of time.

## 21

I am the poet of the Body and I am the poet of the Soul,
The pleasures of heaven are with me and the pains of hell
   are with me,
The first I graft and increase upon myself, the latter I translate into new tongue.

I am the poet of the woman the same as the man,
And I say it is as great to be a woman as to be a man,
And I say there is nothing greater than the mother of men.

I chant the chant of dilation or pride,
We have had ducking and deprecating about enough,
I show that size is only development.

Have you outstript the rest? are you the President?
It is a trifle, they will more than arrive there every one, and
   still pass on.

I am he that walks with the tender and growing night,
I call to the earth and sea half-held by the night.

Press close bare-bosom'd night—press close magnetic nour-
   ishing night!
Night of south winds—night of the large few stars!

Still nodding night—mad naked summer night.

Smile O voluptuous cool-breath'd earth!
Earth of the slumbering and liquid trees!
Earth of departed sunset—earth of the mountains misty-topt!
Earth of the vitreous pour of the full moon just tinged with blue!
Earth of shine and dark mottling the tide of the river!
Earth of the limpid gray of clouds brighter and clearer for my sake!
Far-swooping elbow'd earth—rich apple-blossom'd earth!
Smile, for your lover comes.

Prodigal, you have given me love—therefore I to you give love!
O unspeakable passionate love.

## 22

You sea! I resign myself to you also—I guess what you mean,
I behold from the beach your crooked fingers,
I believe you refuse to go back without feeling of me,
We must have a turn together, I undress, hurry me out of sight of the land,
Cushion me soft, rock me in billowy drowse,
Dash me with amorous wet, I can repay you.

Sea of stretch'd ground-swells,
Sea breathing broad and convulsive breaths,
Sea of the brine of life and of unshovell'd yet always-ready graves,
Howler and scooper of storms, capricious and dainty sea,

I am integral with you, I too am of one phase and of all phases.

Partaker of influx and efflux I, extoller of hate and conciliation,
Extoller of amies and those that sleep in each others' arms.

I am he attesting sympathy,
(Shall I make my list of things in the house and skip the house that supports them?)

I am not the poet of goodness only, I do not decline to be the poet of wickedness also.

What blurt is this about virtue and about vice?
Evil propels me and reform of evil propels me, I stand indifferent,
My gait is no fault-finder's or rejecter's gait,
I moisten the roots of all that has grown.

Did you fear some scrofula out of the unflagging pregnancy?
Did you guess the celestial laws are yet to be work'd over and rectified?

I find one side a balance and the antipedal side a balance,
Soft doctrine as steady help as stable doctrine,
Thoughts and deeds of the present our rouse and early start.

This minute that comes to me over the past decillions,
There is no better than it and now.

What behaved well in the past or behaves well to-day is not such wonder,

The wonder is always and always how there can be a mean man or an infidel.

## 23

Endless unfolding of words of ages!
And mine a word of the modern, the word En-Masse.
A word of the faith that never balks,
Here or henceforward it is all the same to me, I accept Time absolutely.
It alone is without flaw, it alone rounds and completes all,
That mystic baffling wonder alone completes all.
I accept Reality and dare not question it,
Materialism first and last imbuing.
Hurrah for positive science! long live exact demonstration!
Fetch stonecrop mixt with cedar and branches of lilac,
This is the lexicographer, this the chemist, this made a grammar of the old cartouches,
These mariners put the ship through dangerous unknown seas.
This is the geologist, this works with the scalper, and this is a mathematician.
Gentlemen, to you the first honors always!
Your facts are useful, and yet they are not my dwelling,
I but enter by them to an area of my dwelling.
Less the reminders of properties told my words,
And more the reminders they of life untold, and of freedom and extrication,
And make short account of neuters and geldings, and favor men and women fully equipt,
And beat the gong of revolt, and stop with fugitives and them that plot and conspire.

**24**

Walt Whitman, a kosmos, of Manhattan the son,
Turbulent, fleshy, sensual, eating, drinking and breeding,
No sentimentalist, no stander above men and women or
  apart from them,
No more modest than immodest.

Unscrew the locks from the doors!
Unscrew the doors themselves from their jambs!

Whoever degrades another degrades me,
And whatever is done or said returns at last to me.

Through me the afflatus surging and surging, through me
  the current and index.

I speak the pass-word primeval, I give the sign of democracy,
By God! I will accept nothing which all cannot have their
  counterpart of on the same terms.

Through me many long dumb voices,
Voices of the interminable generations of prisoners and slaves,
Voices of the diseas'd and despairing and of thieves and
  dwarfs,
Voices of cycles of preparation and accretion,
And of the threads that connect the stars, and of wombs
  and of the father-stuff,
And of the rights of them the others are down upon,
Of the deform'd, trivial, flat, foolish, despised,
Fog in the air, beetles rolling balls of dung.

Through me forbidden voices,

Voices of sexes and lusts, voices veil'd and I remove the veil,
Voices indecent by me clarified and transfigur'd.


I do not press my fingers across my mouth,
I keep as delicate around the bowels as around the head and
    heart,
Copulation is no more rank to me than death is.
I believe in the flesh and the appetites,
Seeing, hearing, feeling, are miracles, and each part and tag
    of me is a miracle.


Divine am I inside and out, and I make holy whatever I
    touch or am touch'd from,
The scent of these arm-pits aroma finer than prayer,
This head more than churches, bibles, and all the creeds.


If I worship one thing more than another it shall be the
    spread of my own body, or any part of it,
Translucent mould of me it shall be you!
Shaded ledges and rests it shall be you!
Firm masculine colter it shall be you!
Whatever goes to the tilth of me it shall be you!
You my rich blood! your milky stream pale strippings of
    my life!
Breast that presses against other breasts it shall be you!
My brain it shall be your occult convolutions!
Root of wash'd sweet-flag! timorous pond-snipe! nest of
    guarded duplicate eggs! it shall be you!
Mix'd tussled hay of head, beard, brawn, it shall be you!
Trickling sap of maple, fibre of manly wheat, it shall be you!
Sun so generous it shall be you!
Vapors lighting and shading my face it shall be you!

You sweaty brooks and dews it shall be you!
Winds whose soft-tickling genitals rub against me it shall
  be you!
Broad muscular fields, branches of live oak, loving lounger
  in my winding paths, it shall be you!
Hands I have taken, face I have kiss'd, mortal I have ever
  touch'd, it shall be you.

I dote on myself, there is that lot of me and all so luscious,
Each moment and whatever happens thrills me with joy,
I cannot tell how my ankles bend, nor whence the cause of
  my faintest wish,
Nor the cause of the friendship I emit, nor the cause of the
  friendship I take again.

That I walk up my stoop, I pause to consider if it really be,
A morning-glory at my window satisfies me more than the
  metaphysics of books.

To behold the day-break!
The little light fades the immense and diaphanous shadows,
The air tastes good to my palate.

Hefts of the moving world at innocent gambols silently
  rising freshly exuding,
Scooting obliquely high and low.

Something I cannot see puts upward libidinous prongs,
Seas of bright juice suffuse heaven.

The earth by the sky staid with, the daily close of their
  junction,

The heav'd challenge from the east that moment over my head,
The mocking taunt, See then whether you shall be master!

**25**

Dazzling and tremendous how quick the sun-rise would kill
  me,
If I could not now and always send sun-rise out of me.

We also ascend dazzling and tremendous as the sun,
We found our own O my soul in the calm and cool of the
  daybreak.

My voice goes after what my eyes cannot reach,
With the twirl of my tongue I encompass worlds and volumes
  of worlds.

Speech is the twin of my vision, it is unequal to measure
  itself,
It provokes me forever, it says sarcastically,
*Walt you contain enough, why don't you let it out then?*

Come now I will not be tantalized, you conceive too much
  of articulation,
Do you not know O speech how the buds beneath you are
  folded?
Waiting in gloom, protected by frost,
The dirt receding before my prophetical screams,
I underlying causes to balance them at last,
My knowledge my live parts, it keeping tally with the
  meaning of all things,
Happiness, (which whoever hears me let him or her set out
  in search of this day.)

My final merit I refuse you, I refuse putting from me what
   I really am,
Encompass worlds, but never try to encompass me,
I crowd your sleekest and best by simply looking toward
   you.

Writing and talk do not prove me,
I carry the plenum of proof and every thing else in my
   face,
With the hush of my lips I wholly confound the skeptic.

## 26
Now I will do nothing but listen,
To accrue what I hear into this song, to let sounds contribute
   toward it.

I hear bravuras of birds, bustle of growing wheat, gossip of
   flames, clack of sticks cooking my meals,
I hear the sound I love, the sound of the human voice,
I hear all sounds running together, combined, fused or
   following,
Sounds of the city and sounds out of the city, sounds of the
   day and night,
Talkative young ones to those that like them, the loud laugh
   of work-people at their meals,
The angry base of disjointed friendship, the faint tones of
   the sick,
The judge with hands tight to the desk, his pallid lips
   pronouncing a death-sentence,
The heave'e'yo of stevedores unlading ships by the wharves,
   the refrain of the anchor-lifters,
The ring of alarm-bells, the cry of fire, the whirr of swift-

streaking engines and hose-carts with premonitory tinkles
and color'd lights,
The steam-whistle, the solid roll of the train of approaching
cars,
The slow march play'd at the head of the association
marching two and two,
(They go to guard some corpse, the flag-tops are draped
with black muslin.)

I hear the violoncello, ('tis the young man's heart's
complaint,)
I hear the key'd cornet, it glides quickly in through my ears,
It shakes mad-sweet pangs through my belly and breast.

I hear the chorus, it is a grand opera,
Ah this indeed is music—this suits me.

A tenor large and fresh as the creation fills me,
The orbic flex of his mouth is pouring and filling me full.

I hear the train'd soprano (what work with hers is this?)
The orchestra whirls me wider than Uranus flies,
It wrenches such ardors from me I did not know I possess'd
them,
It sails me, I dab with bare feet, they are lick'd by the indo-
lent waves,
I am cut by bitter and angry hail, I lose my breath,
Steep'd amid honey'd morphine, my windpipe throttled in
fakes of death,
At length let up again to feel the puzzle of puzzles,
And that we call Being.

## 27

To be in any form, what is that?

(Round and round we go, all of us, and ever come back
  thither,)

If nothing lay more develop'd the quahaug in its callous
  shell were enough.

Mine is no callous shell,

I have instant conductors all over me whether I pass or
  stop,

They seize every object and lead it harmlessly through me.

I merely stir, press, feel with my fingers, and am happy,

To touch my person to some one else's is about as much as
  I can stand.

## 28

Is this then a touch? quivering me to a new identity,

Flames and ether making a rush for my veins,

Treacherous tip of me reaching and crowding to help them,

My flesh and blood playing out lightning to strike what is
  hardly different from myself,

On all sides prurient provokers stiffening my limbs,

Straining the udder of my heart for its withheld drip,

Behaving licentious toward me, taking no denial,

Depriving me of my best as for a purpose,

Unbuttoning my clothes, holding me by the bare waist,

Deluding my confusion with the calm of the sunlight and
  pasture-fields,

Immodestly sliding the fellow-senses away,

They bribed to swap off with touch and go and graze at
  the edges of me,

No consideration, no regard for my draining strength or my
    anger,
Fetching the rest of the herd around to enjoy them a while,
Then all uniting to stand on a headland and worry me.

The sentries desert every other part of me,
They have left me helpless to a red marauder,
They all come to the headland to witness and assist against
    me.

I am given up by traitors,
I talk wildly, I have lost my wits, I and nobody else am the
    greatest traitor,
I went myself first to the headland, my own hands carried
    me there.

You villain touch! what are you doing? my breath is tight
    in its throat,
Unclench your floodgates, you are too much for me.

## 29

Blind loving wrestling touch, sheath'd hooded sharp-tooth'd
    touch!
Did it make you ache so, leaving me?

Parting track'd by arriving, perpetual payment of perpetual
    loan,
Rich showering rain, and recompense richer afterward.

Sprouts take and accumulate, stand by the curb prolific and
    vital,
Landscapes projected masculine, full-sized and golden.

**30**

All truths wait in all things,
They neither hasten their own delivery nor resist it,
They do not need the obstetric forceps of the surgeon,
The insignificant is as big to me as any,
(What is less or more than a touch?)

Logic and sermons never convince,
The damp of the night drives deeper into my soul.

(Only what proves itself to every man and woman is so,
Only what nobody denies is so.)

A minute and a drop of me settle my brain,
I believe the soggy clods shall become lovers and lamps,
And a compend of compends is the meat of a man or
  woman,
And a summit and flower there is the feeling they have for
  each other,
And they are to branch boundlessly out of that lesson until
  it becomes omnific,
And until one and all shall delight us, and we them.

**31**

I believe a leaf of grass is no less than the journey work of
  the stars,
And the pismire is equally perfect, and a grain of sand, and
  the egg of the wren,
And the tree-toad is a chef-d'oeuvre for the highest,
And the running blackberry would adorn the parlors of
  heaven,

And the narrowest hinge in my hand puts to scorn all
    machinery,
And the cow crunching with depress'd head surpasses any
    statue,
And a mouse is miracle enough to stagger sextillions of
    infidels.

I find I incorporate gneiss, coal, long-threaded moss, fruits,
    grains, esculent roots,
And am stucco'd with quadrupeds and birds all over,
And have distanced what is behind me for good reasons,
But call any thing back again when I desire it.

In vain the speeding or shyness,
In vain the plutonic rocks send their old heat against my
    approach,
In vain the mastodon retreats beneath its own powder'd bones,
In vain objects stand leagues off and assume manifold
    shapes,
In vain the ocean settling in hollows and the great monsters
    lying low,
In vain the buzzard houses herself with the sky,
In vain the snake slides through the creepers and logs,
In vain the elk takes to the inner passes of the woods,
In vain the razor-bill'd auk sails far north to Labrador,
I follow quickly, I ascend to the nest in the fissure of the cliff.

## 32

I think I could turn and live with animals, they are so placid
    and self-contain'd,
I stand and look at them long and long.

They do not sweat and whine about their condition,
They do not lie awake in the dark and weep for their
sins,
They do not make me sick discussing their duty to God,
Not one is dissatisfied, not one is demented with the mania
of owning things,
Not one kneels to another, nor to his kind that lived thou-
sands of years ago,
Not one is respectable or unhappy over the whole earth.

So they show their relations to me and I accept them,
They bring me tokens of myself, they evince them plainly
in their possession.

I wonder where they get those tokens,
Did I pass that way huge times ago and negligently drop
them?
Myself moving forward then and now and forever,
Gathering and showing more always and with velocity,
Infinite and omnigenous, and the like of these among them,
Not too exclusive toward the reachers of my remem-
brancers,
Picking out here one that I love, and now go with him on
brotherly terms.

A gigantic beauty of a stallion, fresh and responsive to my
caresses,
Head high in the forehead, wide between the ears,
Limbs glossy and supple, tail dusting the ground,
Eyes full of sparkling wickedness, ears finely cut, flexibly
moving.

His nostrils dilate as my heels embrace him,
His well-built limbs tremble with pleasure as we race around
   and return.

I but use you a minute, then I resign you, stallion,
Why do I need your paces when I myself out-gallop them?
Even as I stand or sit passing faster than you.

## 33

Space and Time! now I see it is true, what I guess'd at,
What I guess'd when I loaf'd on the grass,
What I guess'd while I lay alone in my bed,
And again as I walk'd the beach under the paling stars of
   the morning.

My ties and ballasts leave me, my elbows rest in sea-gaps,
I skirt sierras, my palms cover continents,
I am afoot with my vision.

By the city's quadrangular houses—in log huts, camping
   with lumber-men,
Along the ruts of the turnpike, along the dry gulch and
   rivulet bed,
Weeding my onion-patch or hosing rows of carrots and
   parsnips, crossing savannas, trailing in forests,
Prospecting, gold-digging, girdling the trees of a new purchase,
Scorch'd ankle-deep by the hot sand, hauling my boat down
   the shallow river,
Where the panther walks to and fro on a limb overhead,
   where the buck turns furiously at the hunter,
Where the rattlesnake suns his flabby length on a rock, where
   the otter is feeding on fish,

Where the alligator in his tough pimples sleeps by the bayou,

Where the black bear is searching for roots or honey, where the beaver pats the mud with his paddle-shaped tall;

Over the growing sugar, over the yellow-flower'd cotton plant, over the rice in its low moist field,

Over the sharp-peak'd farm house, with its scallop'd scum and slender shoots from the gutters,

Over the western persimmon, over the long-leav'd corn, over the delicate blue-flower flax,

Over the white and brown buckwheat, a hummer and buzzer there with the rest,

Over the dusky green of the rye as it ripples and shades in the breeze;

Scaling mountains, pulling myself cautiously up, holding on by low scragged limbs,

Walking the path worn in the grass and beat through the leaves of the brush,

Where the quail is whistling betwixt the woods and the wheat-lot,

Where the bat flies in the Seventh-month eve, where the great goldbug drops through the dark,

Where the brook puts out of the roots of the old tree and flows to the meadow,

Where cattle stand and shake away flies with the tremulous shuddering of their hides,

Where the cheese-cloth hangs in the kitchen, where and-irons straddle the hearth-slab, where cobwebs fall in festoons from the rafters;

Where trip-hammers crash, where the press is whirling its cylinders,

Wherever the human heart beats with terrible throes under its ribs,

Where the pear-shaped balloon is floating aloft, (floating in
it myself and looking composedly down,)
Where the life-car is drawn on the slip-noose, where the
heat hatches pale-green eggs in the dented sand,
Where the she-whale swims with her calf and never forsakes
it,
Where the steam-ship trails hind-ways its long pennant of
smoke,
Where the fin of the shark cuts like a black chip out of the
water,
Where the half-burn'd brig is riding on unknown currents,
Where shells grow to her slimy deck, where the dead are
corrupting below;
Where the dense-starr'd flag is borne at the head of the
regiments,
Approaching Manhattan up by the long-stretching island,
Under Niagara, the cataract falling like a veil over my coun-
tenance,
Upon a door-step, upon the horse-block of hard wood
outside,
Upon the race-course, or enjoying picnics or jigs or a good
game of base-ball,
At he-festivals, with blackguard gibes, ironical license, bull-
dances, drinking, laughter,
At the cider-mill tasting the sweets of the brown mash,
sucking the juice through a straw,
At apple-peelings wanting kisses for all the red fruit I find,
At musters, beach-parties, friendly bees, huskings, house-
raisings;
Where the mocking-bird sounds his delicious gurgles,
cackles, screams, weeps,
Where the hay-rick stands in the barn-yard, where the

dry-stalks are scatter'd, where the brood-cow waits in the hovel,
Where the bull advances to do his masculine work, where the stud to the mare, where the cock is treading the hen,
Where the heifers browse, where geese nip their food with short jerks,
Where sun-down shadows lengthen over the limitless and lonesome prairie,
Where herds of buffalo make a crawling spread of the square miles far and near,
Where the humming-bird shimmers, where the neck of the long-lived swan is curving and winding,
Where the laughing-gull scoots by the shore, where she laughs her near-human laugh,
Where bee-hives range on a gray bench in the garden half hid by the high weeds,
Where band-neck'd partridges roost in a ring on the ground with their heads out,
Where burial coaches enter the arch'd gates of a cemetery,
Where winter wolves bark amid wastes of snow and icicled trees,
Where the yellow-crown'd heron comes to the edge of the marsh at night and feeds upon small crabs,
Where the splash of swimmers and divers cools the warm noon,
Where the katy-did works her chromatic reed on the walnut-tree over the well,
Through patches of citrons and cucumbers with silver-wired leaves,
Through the salt-lick or orange glade, or under conical firs,
Through the gymnasium, through the curtain'd saloon, through the office or public hall;

Pleas'd with the native and pleas'd with the foreign, pleas'd
  with the new and old,
Pleas'd with the homely woman as well as the handsome,
Pleas'd with the quakeress as she puts off her bonnet and
  talks melodiously,
Pleas'd with the tune of the choir of the whitewash'd church,
Pleas'd with the earnest words of the sweating Methodist
  preacher, impress'd seriously at the camp-meeting;
Looking in at the shop-windows of Broadway the whole fore-
  noon, flatting the flesh of my nose on the thick plate glass,
Wandering the same afternoon with my face turn'd up to
  the clouds, or down a lane or along the beach,
My right and left arms round the sides of two friends, and
  I in the middle;
Coming home with the silent and dark-cheek'd bush-boy,
  (behind me he rides at the drape of the day,)
Far from the settlements studying the print of animals' feet,
  or the moccasin print,
By the cot in the hospital reaching lemonade to a feverish
  patient,
Nigh the coffin'd corpse when all is still, examining with a
  candle;
Voyaging to every port to dicker and adventure,
Hurrying with the modern crowd as eager and fickle as
  any,
Hot toward one I hate, ready in my madness to knife him,
Solitary at midnight in my back yard, my thoughts gone
  from me a long while,
Walking the old hills of Judaea with the beautiful gentle
  God by my side,
Speeding through space, speeding through heaven and the
  stars,

Speeding amid the seven satellites and the broad ring, and
  the diameter of eighty thousand miles,
Speeding with tail'd meteors, throwing fire-balls like the
  rest,
Carrying the crescent child that carries its own full mother
  in its belly,
Storming, enjoying, planning, loving, cautioning,
Backing and filling, appearing and disappearing,
I tread day and night such roads.

I visit the orchards of spheres and look at the product,
And look at quintillions ripen'd and look at quintillions
  green.

I fly those flights of a fluid and swallowing soul,
My course runs below the soundings of plummets.

I help myself to material and immaterial,
No guard can shut me off, no law prevent me.

I anchor my ship for a little while only,
My messengers continually cruise away or bring their returns
  to me.

I go hunting polar furs and the seal, leaping chasms with a
  pike-pointed staff, clinging to topples of brittle and blue.

I ascend to the foretruck,
I take my place late at night in the crow's-nest,
We sail the arctic sea, it is plenty light enough,
Through the clear atmosphere I stretch around on the
  wonderful beauty,

The enormous masses of ice pass me and I pass them, the
scenery is plain in all directions,
The white-topt mountains show in the distance, I fling out
my fancies toward them,
We are approaching some great battle-field in which we are
soon to be engaged,
We pass the colossal outposts of the encampment, we pass
with still feet and caution,
Or we are entering by the suburbs some vast and ruin'd city,
The blocks and fallen architecture more than all the living
cities of the globe.

I am a free companion, I bivouac by invading watchfires,
I turn the bridegroom out of bed and stay with the bride
myself,
I tighten her all night to my thighs and lips.

My voice is the wife's voice, the screech by the rail of the
stairs,
They fetch my man's body up dripping and drown'd.

I understand the large hearts of heroes,
The courage of present times and all times,
How the skipper saw the crowded and rudderless wreck of
the steamship, and Death chasing it up and down the storm,
How he knuckled tight and gave not back an inch, and was
faithful of days and faithful of nights,
And chalk'd in large letters on a board, Be of good cheer,
we will not desert you;
How he follow'd with them and tack'd with them three days
and would not give it up,
How he saved the drifting company at last,

How the lank loose-gown'd women look'd when boated
  from the side of their prepared graves,
How the silent old-faced infants and the lifted sick, and the
  sharp-lipp'd unshaved men;
All this I swallow, it tastes good, I like it well, it becomes mine,
I am the man, I suffer'd, I was there.


The disdain and calmness of martyrs,
The mother of old, condemn'd for a witch, burnt with dry
  wood, her children gazing on,
The hounded slave that flags in the race, leans by the fence,
  blowing, cover'd with sweat,
The twinges that sting like needles his legs and neck, the
  murderous buckshot and the bullets,
All these I feel or am.


I am the hounded slave, I wince at the bite of the dogs,
Hell and despair are upon me, crack and again crack the
  marksmen,
I clutch the rails of the fence, my gore dribs, thinn'd with
  the ooze of my skin,
I fall on the weeds and stones,
The riders spur their unwilling horses, haul close,
Taunt my dizzy ears and beat me violently over the head
  with whip-stocks.


Agonies are one of my changes of garments,
I do not ask the wounded person how he feels, I myself
  become the wounded person,
My hurts turn livid upon me as I lean on a cane and observe.


I am the mash'd fireman with breast-bone broken,

Tumbling walls buried me in their debris,
Heat and smoke I inspired, I heard the yelling shouts of my
comrades,
I heard the distant click of their picks and shovels,
They have clear'd the beams away, they tenderly lift me forth.

I lie in the night air in my red shirt, the pervading hush is
for my sake,
Painless after all I lie exhausted but not so unhappy,
White and beautiful are the faces around me, the heads are
bared of their fire-caps,
The kneeling crowd fades with the light of the torches.

Distant and dead resuscitate,
They show as the dial or move as the hands of me, I am
the clock myself.

I am an old artillerist, I tell of my fort's bombardment,
I am there again.

Again the long roll of the drummers,
Again the attacking cannon, mortars,
Again to my listening ears the cannon responsive.

I take part, I see and hear the whole,
The cries, curses, roar, the plaudits for well-aim'd shots,
The ambulanza slowly passing trailing its red drip,
Workmen searching after damages, making indispensable
repairs,
The fall of grenades through the rent roof, the fan-shaped
explosion,
The whizz of limbs, heads, stone, wood, iron, high in the air.

Again gurgles the mouth of my dying general, he furiously
   waves with his hand,
He gasps through the clot *Mind not me—mind—the entrenchments.*


**34**
Now I tell what I knew in Texas in my early youth,
(I tell not the fall of Alamo,
Not one escaped to tell the fall of Alamo,
The hundred and fifty are dumb yet at Alamo,)
'Tis the tale of the murder in cold blood of four hundred
   and twelve young men.


Retreating they had form'd in a hollow square with their
   baggage for breastworks,
Nine hundred lives out of the surrounding enemies, nine
   times their number, was the price they took in advance,
Their colonel was wounded and their ammunition gone,
They treated for an honorable capitulation, receiv'd writing
   and seal, gave up their arms and march'd back prisoners
   of war.


They were the glory of the race of rangers,
Matchless with horse, rifle, song, supper, courtship,
Large, turbulent, generous, handsome, proud, and affectionate,
Bearded, sunburnt, drest in the free costume of hunters,
Not a single one over thirty years of age.


The second First-day morning they were brought out in
   squads and massacred, it was beautiful early summer,
The work commenced about five o'clock and was over by
   eight.

None obey'd the command to kneel,

Some made a mad and helpless rush, some stood stark and
  straight,

A few fell at once, shot in the temple or heart, the living
  and dead lay together,

The maim'd and mangled dug in the dirt, the new-comers
  saw them there,

Some half-kill'd attempted to crawl away,

These were despatch'd with bayonets or batter'd with the
  blunts of muskets,

A youth not seventeen years old seiz'd his assassin till two
  more came to release him,

The three were all torn and cover'd with the boy's blood.


At eleven o'clock began the burning of the bodies;

That is the tale of the murder of the four hundred and twelve
  young men.


**35**

Would you hear of an old-time sea-fight?

Would you learn who won by the light of the moon and
  stars?

List to the yarn, as my grandmother's father the sailor told
  it to me.


Our foe was no skulk in his ship I tell you, (said he,)

His was the surly English pluck, and there is no tougher or
  truer, and never was, and never will be;

Along the lower'd eve he came horribly raking us.


We closed with him, the yards entangled, the cannon touch'd,

My captain lash'd fast with his own hands.

We had receiv'd some eighteen pound shots under the water,
On our lower-gun-deck two large pieces had burst at the
first fire, killing all around and blowing up overhead.

Fighting at sun-down, fighting at dark,
Ten o'clock at night, the full moon well up, our leaks on
the gain, and five feet of water reported,
The master-at-arms loosing the prisoners confined in the
after-hold to give them a chance for themselves.

The transit to and from the magazine is now stopt by the
sentinels,
They see so many strange faces they do not know whom to
trust.

Our frigate takes fire,
The other asks if we demand quarter?
If our colors are struck and the fighting done?

Now I laugh content, for I hear the voice of my little captain,
*We have not struck*, he composedly cries, *we have just begun our part
of the fighting.*

Only three guns are in use,
One is directed by the captain himself against the enemy's
main-mast,
Two well serv'd with grape and canister silence his musketry
and clear his decks.

The tops alone second the fire of this little battery, especially
the main-top,
They hold out bravely during the whole of the action.

Not a moment's cease,

The leaks gain fast on the pumps, the fire eats toward the
powder-magazine.

One of the pumps has been shot away, it is generally thought
we are sinking.

Serene stands the little captain,

He is not hurried, his voice is neither high nor low,

His eyes give more light to us than our battle-lanterns.

Toward twelve there in the beams of the moon they surrender
to us.

### 36

Stretch'd and still lies the midnight,

Two great hulls motionless on the breast of the darkness,

Our vessel riddled and slowly sinking, preparations to pass
to the one we have conquer'd,

The captain on the quarter-deck coldly giving his orders
through a countenance white as a sheet,

Near by the corpse of the child that serv'd in the cabin,

The dead face of an old salt with long white hair and carefully curl'd whiskers,

The flames spite of all that can be done flickering aloft and
below,

The husky voices of the two or three officers yet fit for duty,

Formless stacks of bodies and bodies by themselves, dabs of
flesh upon the masts and spars,

Cut of cordage, dangle of rigging, slight shock of the soothe
of waves,

Black and impassive guns, litter of powder-parcels, strong scent,

A few large stars overhead, silent and mournful shining,
Delicate sniffs of sea-breeze, smells of sedgy grass and fields
   by the shore, death-messages given in charge to survivors,
The hiss of the surgeon's knife, the gnawing teeth of his saw,
Wheeze, cluck, swash of falling blood, short wild scream,
   and long, dull, tapering groan,
These so, these irretrievable.

### 37

You laggards there on guard! look to your arms!
In at the conquer'd doors they crowd! I am possess'd!
Embody all presences outlaw'd or suffering,
See myself in prison shaped like another man,
And feel the dull unintermitted pain.

For me the keepers of convicts shoulder their carbines and
   keep watch,
It is I let out in the morning and barr'd at night.

Not a mutineer walks handcuff'd to jail but I am handcuff'd
   to him and walk by his side,
(I am less the jolly one there, and more the silent one with
   sweat on my twitching lips.)

Not a youngster is taken for larceny but I go up too, and
   am tried and sentenced.

Not a cholera patient lies at the last gasp but I also lie at
   the last gasp,
My face is ash-color'd, my sinews gnarl, away from me
   people retreat.

Askers embody themselves in me and I am embodied in
    them,
I project my hat, sit shame-faced, and beg.

**38**
Enough! enough! enough!
Somehow I have been stunn'd. Stand back!
Give me a little time beyond my cuff'd head, slumbers,
    dreams, gaping,
I discover myself on the verge of a usual mistake.

That I could forget the mockers and insults!
That I could forget the trickling tears and the blows of the
    bludgeons and hammers!
That I could look with a separate look on my own crucifixion
    and bloody crowning.

I remember now,
I resume the overstaid fraction,
The grave of rock multiplies what has been confided to it,
    or to any graves,
Corpses rise, gashes heal, fastenings roll from me.

I troop forth replenish'd with supreme power, one of an
    average unending procession,
Inland and sea-coast we go, and pass all boundary lines,
Our swift ordinances on their way over the whole earth,
The blossoms we wear in our hats the growth of thousands
    of years.

Eleves, I salute you! come forward!
Continue your annotations, continue your questionings.

## 39

The friendly and flowing savage, who is he?
Is he waiting for civilization, or past it and mastering it?


Is he some Southwesterner rais'd out-doors? is he Kanadian?
Is he from the Mississippi country? Iowa, Oregon, California?
The mountains? prairie-life, bush-life? or sailor from the sea?


Wherever he goes men and women accept and desire him,
They desire he should like them, touch them, speak to them,
  stay with them.


Behavior lawless as snow-flakes, words simple as grass,
  uncomb'd head, laughter, and naivete,
Slow-stepping feet, common features, common modes and
  emanations,
They descend in new forms from the tips of his fingers,
They are wafted with the odor of his body or breath, they
  fly out of the glance of his eyes.

## 40

Flaunt of the sunshine I need not your bask—lie over!
You light surfaces only, I force surfaces and depths also.


Earth! you seem to look for something at my hands,
Say, old top-knot, what do you want?


Man or woman, I might tell how I like you, but cannot,
And might tell what it is in me and what it is in you, but
  cannot,
And might tell that pining I have, that pulse of my nights
  and days.

Behold, I do not give lectures or a little charity,
When I give I give myself.

You there, impotent, loose in the knees,
Open your scarf'd chops till I blow grit within you,
Spread your palms and lift the flaps of your pockets,
I am not to be denied, I compel, I have stores plenty and
    to spare,
And any thing I have I bestow.

I do not ask who you are, that is not important to me,
You can do nothing and be nothing but what I will infold
    you.

To cotton-field drudge or cleaner of privies I lean,
On his right cheek I put the family kiss,
And in my soul I swear I never will deny him.

On women fit for conception I start bigger and nimbler
    babes.
(This day I am jetting the stuff of far more arrogant republics.)

To any one dying, thither I speed and twist the knob of the
    door.
Turn the bed-clothes toward the foot of the bed,
Let the physician and the priest go home.

I seize the descending man and raise him with resistless
    will,
O despairer, here is my neck,
By God, you shall not go down! hang your whole weight
    upon me.

I dilate you with tremendous breath, I buoy you up,
Every room of the house do I fill with an arm'd force,
Lovers of me, bafflers of graves.

Sleep—I and they keep guard all night,
Not doubt, not decease shall dare to lay finger upon you,
I have embraced you, and henceforth possess you to myself,
And when you rise in the morning you will find what I tell
    you is so.


**41**

I am he bringing help for the sick as they pant on their
    backs,
And for strong upright men I bring yet more needed help.

I heard what was said of the universe,
Heard it and heard it of several thousand years;
It is middling well as far as it goes—but is that all?

Magnifying and applying come I,
Outbidding at the start the old cautious hucksters,
Taking myself the exact dimensions of Jehovah,
Lithographing Kronos, Zeus his son, and Hercules his
    grandson,
Buying drafts of Osiris, Isis, Belus, Brahma, Buddha,
In my portfolio placing Manito loose, Allah on a leaf, the
    crucifix engraved,
With Odin and the hideous-faced Mexitli and every idol and
    image,
Taking them all for what they are worth and not a cent
    more,
Admitting they were alive and did the work of their days,

(They bore mites as for unfledg'd birds who have now to
rise and fly and sing for themselves,)
Accepting the rough deific sketches to fill out better in myself,
bestowing them freely on each man and woman I see,
Discovering as much or more in a framer framing a house,
Putting higher claims for him there with his roll'd-up sleeves
driving the mallet and chisel,
Not objecting to special revelations, considering a curl of
smoke or a hair on the back of my hand just as curious
as any revelation,
Lads ahold of fire-engines and hook-and-ladder ropes no
less to me than the gods of the antique wars,
Minding their voices peal through the crash of destruction,
Their brawny limbs passing safe over charr'd laths, their
white foreheads whole and unhurt out of the flames;
By the mechanic's wife with her babe at her nipple inter-
ceding for every person born,
Three scythes at harvest whizzing in a row from three lusty
angels with shirts bagg'd out at their waists,
The snag-tooth'd hostler with red hair redeeming sins past
and to come,
Selling all he possesses, traveling on foot to fee lawyers
for his brother and sit by him while he is tried for
forgery;
What was strewn in the amplest strewing the square rod
about me, and not filling the square rod then,
The bull and the bug never worshipp'd half enough,
Dung and dirt more admirable than was dream'd,
The supernatural of no account, myself waiting my time to
be one of the supremes,
The day getting ready for me when I shall do as much good
as the best, and be as prodigious;

By my life-lumps! becoming already a creator,
Putting myself here and now to the ambush'd womb of the
  shadows.

**42**

A call in the midst of the crowd,
My own voice, orotund sweeping and final.

Come my children,
Come my boys and girls, my women, household and inti-
  mates,
Now the performer launches his nerve, he has pass'd his
  prelude on the reeds within.

Easily written loose-finger'd chords—I feel the thrum of
  your climax and close.

My head slues round on my neck,
Music rolls, but not from the organ,
Folks are around me, but they are no household of mine.

Ever the hard unsunk ground,
Ever the eaters and drinkers, ever the upward and downward
  sun, ever the air and the ceaseless tides,
Ever myself and my neighbors, refreshing, wicked, real,
Ever the old inexplicable query, ever that thorn'd thumb,
  that breath of itches and thirsts,
Ever the vexer's *hoot! hoot!* till we find where the sly one hides
  and bring him forth,
Ever love, ever the sobbing liquid of life,
Ever the bandage under the chin, ever the trestles of death.

Here and there with dimes on the eyes walking,
To feed the greed of the belly the brains liberally spooning,
Tickets buying, taking, selling, but in to the feast never once
    going,
Many sweating, ploughing, thrashing, and then the chaff for
    payment receiving,
A few idly owning, and they the wheat continually claiming.

This is the city and I am one of the citizens,
Whatever interests the rest interests me, politics, wars,
    markets, newspapers, schools,
The mayor and councils, banks, tariffs, steamships, factories,
    stocks, stores, real estate and personal estate.

The little plentiful manikins skipping around in collars and
    tail'd coats,
I am aware who they are, (they are positively not worms or
    fleas,)
I acknowledge the duplicates of myself, the weakest and
    shallowest is deathless with me,
What I do and say the same waits for them,
Every thought that flounders in me the same flounders in
    them.

I know perfectly well my own egotism,
Know my omnivorous lines and must not write any less,
And would fetch you whoever you are flush with myself.

Not words of routine this song of mine,
But abruptly to question, to leap beyond yet nearer bring;
This printed and bound book—but the printer and the
    printing-office boy?

The well-taken photographs—but your wife or friend close
and solid in your arms?
The black ship mail'd with iron, her mighty guns in her
turrets—but the pluck of the captain and engineers?
In the houses the dishes and fare and furniture—but the
host and hostess, and the look out of their eyes?
The sky up there—yet here or next door, or across the way?
The saints and sages in history—but you yourself?
Sermons, creeds, theology—but the fathomless human brain,
And what is reason? and what is love? and what is life?


## 43

I do not despise you priests, all time, the world over,
My faith is the greatest of faiths and the least of faiths,
Enclosing worship ancient and modern and all between
ancient and modern,
Believing I shall come again upon the earth after five thou-
sand years,
Waiting responses from oracles, honoring the gods, saluting
the sun,
Making a fetich of the first rock or stump, powowing with
sticks in the circle of obis,
Helping the llama or brahmin as he trims the lamps of the
idols,
Dancing yet through the streets in a phallic procession, rapt
and austere in the woods a gymnosophist,
Drinking mead from the skull-cap, to Shastas and Vedas
admirant, minding the Koran,
Walking the teokallis, spotted with gore from the stone and
knife, beating the serpent-skin drum,
Accepting the Gospels, accepting him that was crucified,
knowing assuredly that he is divine,

To the mass kneeling or the puritan's prayer rising, or sitting
    patiently in a pew,
Ranting and frothing in my insane crisis, or waiting dead-
    like till my spirit arouses me,
Looking forth on pavement and land, or outside of pavement
    and land,
Belonging to the winders of the circuit of circuits.

One of that centripetal and centrifugal gang I turn and talk
    like man leaving charges before a journey.

Down-hearted doubters dull and excluded,
Frivolous, sullen, moping, angry, affected, dishearten'd, athe-
    istical,
I know every one of you, I know the sea of torment, doubt,
    despair and unbelief.

How the flukes splash!
How they contort rapid as lightning, with spasms and spouts
    of blood!

Be at peace bloody flukes of doubters and sullen mopers,
I take my place among you as much as among any,
The past is the push of you, me, all, precisely the same,
And what is yet untried and afterward is for you, me, all,
    precisely the same.

I do not know what is untried and afterward,
But I know it will in its turn prove sufficient, and cannot fail.

Each who passes is consider'd, each who stops is consider'd,
    not single one can it fall.

It cannot fall the young man who died and was buried,
Nor the young woman who died and was put by his side,
Nor the little child that peep'd in at the door, and then drew
  back and was never seen again,
Nor the old man who has lived without purpose, and feels
  it with bitterness worse than gall,
Nor him in the poor house tubercled by rum and the bad
  disorder,
Nor the numberless slaughter'd and wreck'd, nor the brutish
  koboo call'd the ordure of humanity,
Nor the sacs merely floating with open mouths for food to
  slip in,
Nor any thing in the earth, or down in the oldest graves of
  the earth,
Nor any thing in the myriads of spheres, nor the myriads
  of myriads that inhabit them,
Nor the present, nor the least wisp that is known.

**44**
It is time to explain myself—let us stand up.

What is known I strip away,
I launch all men and women forward with me into the
  Unknown.

The clock indicates the moment—but what does eternity
  indicate?

We have thus far exhausted trillions of winters and
  summers,
There are trillions ahead, and trillions ahead of them.

Births have brought us richness and variety,
And other births will bring us richness and variety.

I do not call one greater and one smaller,
That which fills its period and place is equal to any.

Were mankind murderous or jealous upon you, my brother,
    my sister?
I am sorry for you, they are not murderous or jealous upon
    me,
All has been gentle with me, I keep no account with lamen-
    tation,
(What have I to do with lamentation?)

I am an acme of things accomplish'd, and I an encloser of
    things to be.

My feet strike an apex of the apices of the stairs,
On every step bunches of ages, and larger bunches between
    the steps,
All below duly travel'd, and still I mount and mount.

Rise after rise bow the phantoms behind me,
Afar down I see the huge first Nothing, I know I was even
    there,
I waited unseen and always, and slept through the lethargic
    mist,
And took my time, and took no hurt from the fetid carbon.

Long I was hugg'd close—long and long.

Immense have been the preparations for me,

Faithful and friendly the arms that have help'd me.

Cycles ferried my cradle, rowing and rowing like cheerful
  boatmen,
For room to me stars kept aside in their own rings,
They sent influences to look after what was to hold me.

Before I was born out of my mother generations guided me,
My embryo has never been torpid, nothing could overlay it.

For it the nebula cohered to an orb,
The long slow strata piled to rest it on,
Vast vegetables gave it sustenance,
Monstrous sauroids transported it in their mouths and
  deposited it with care.

All forces have been steadily employ'd to complete and
  delight me,
Now on this spot I stand with my robust soul.

## 45
O span of youth! ever-push'd elasticity!
O manhood, balanced, florid and full.

My lovers suffocate me,
Crowding my lips, thick in the pores of my skin,
Jostling me through streets and public halls, coming naked
  to me at night,
Crying by day, Ahoy! from the rocks of the river, swinging
  and chirping over my head,
Calling my name from flower-beds, vines, tangled underbrush,
Lighting on every moment of my life,

Bussing my body with soft balsamic busses,
Noiselessly passing handfuls out of their hearts and giving
them to be mine.

Old age superbly rising! O welcome, ineffable grace of dying
days!

Every condition promulges not only itself, it promulges what
grows after and out of itself,
And the dark hush promulges as much as any.

I open my scuttle at night and see the far-sprinkled
systems,
And all I see multiplied as high as I can cipher edge but the
rim of the farther systems.

Wider and wider they spread, expanding, always expanding,
Outward and outward and forever outward.

My sun has his sun and round him obediently wheels,
He joins with his partners a group of superior circuit,
And greater sets follow, making specks of the greatest inside
them.

There is no stoppage and never can be stoppage,
If I, you, and the worlds, and all beneath or upon their
surfaces, were this moment reduced back to a pallid float,
it would not avail the long run,
We should surely bring up again where we now stand,
And surely go as much farther, and then farther and farther.

A few quadrillions of eras, a few octillions of cubic leagues,

do not hazard the span or make it impatient,
They are but parts, any thing is but a part.

See ever so far, there is limitless space outside of that,
Count ever so much, there is limitless time around that.

My rendezvous is appointed, it is certain,
The Lord will be there and wait till I come on perfect terms,
The great Camerado, the lover true for whom I pine will
  be there.

**46**

I know I have the best of time and space, and was never
  measured and never will be measured.

I tramp a perpetual journey, (come listen all!)
My signs are a rain-proof coat, good shoes, and a staff cut
  from the woods,
No friend of mine takes his ease in my chair,
I have no chair, no church, no philosophy,
I lead no man to a dinner-table, library, exchange,
But each man and each woman of you I lead upon a knoll,
My left hand hooking you round the waist,
My right hand pointing to landscapes of continents and the
  public road.

Not I, not any one else can travel that road for you,
You must travel it for yourself.

It is not far, it is within reach,
Perhaps you have been on it since you were born and did
  not know,

Perhaps it is everywhere on water and on land.

Shoulder your duds dear son, and I will mine, and let us
 hasten forth,
Wonderful cities and free nations we shall fetch as we go.

If you tire, give me both burdens, and rest the chuff of your
 hand on my hip,
And in due time you shall repay the same service to me,
For after we start we never lie by again.

This day before dawn I ascended a hill and look'd at the
 crowded heaven,
And I said to my spirit *When we become the enfolders of those orbs,
 and the pleasure and knowledge of every thing in them, shall we be fill'd
 and satisfied then?*
And my spirit said *No, we but level that lift to pass and continue beyond.*

You are also asking me questions and I hear you,
I answer that I cannot answer, you must find out for yourself.

Sit a while dear son,
Here are biscuits to eat and here is milk to drink,
But as soon as you sleep and renew yourself in sweet clothes,
 I kiss you with a good-by kiss and open the gate for your
 egress hence.

Long enough have you dream'd contemptible dreams,
Now I wash the gum from your eyes,
You must habit yourself to the dazzle of the light and of
 every moment of your life.

Long have you timidly waded holding a plank by the shore,
Now I will you to be a bold swimmer,
To jump off in the midst of the sea, rise again, nod to me,
    shout, and laughingly dash with your hair.

## 47

I am the teacher of athletes,
He that by me spreads a wider breast than my own proves
    the width of my own,
He most honors my style who learns under it to destroy the
    teacher.


The boy I love, the same becomes a man not through derived
    power, but in his own right,
Wicked rather than virtuous out of conformity or fear,
Fond of his sweetheart, relishing well his steak,
Unrequited love or a slight cutting him worse than sharp
    steel cuts,
First-rate to ride, to fight, to hit the bull's eye, to sail a skiff,
    to sing a song or play on the banjo,
Preferring scars and the beard and faces pitted with small-pox
    over all latherers,
And those well-tann'd to those that keep out of the sun.


I teach straying from me, yet who can stray from me?
I follow you whoever you are from the present hour,
My words itch at your ears till you understand them.


I do not say these things for a dollar or to fill up the time
    while I wait for a boat,
(It is you talking just as much as myself, I act as the tongue
    of you,

Tied in your mouth, in mine it begins to be loosen'd.)

I swear I will never again mention love or death inside a
    house,
And I swear I will never translate myself at all, only to him
    or her who privately stays with me in the open air.

If you would understand me go to the heights or water-shore,
The nearest gnat is an explanation, and a drop or motion
    of waves key,
The maul, the oar, the hand-saw, second my words.

No shutter'd room or school can commune with me,
But roughs and little children better than they.

The young mechanic is closest to me, he knows me well,
The woodman that takes his axe and jug with him shall take
    me with him all day,
The farm-boy ploughing in the field feels good at the sound
    of my voice,
In vessels that sail my words sail, I go with fishermen and
    seamen and love them.

The soldier camp'd or upon the march is mine,
On the night ere the pending battle many seek me, and I
    do not fail them,
On that solemn night (it may be their last) those that know
    me seek me.

My face rubs to the hunter's face when he lies down alone
    in his blanket,
The driver thinking of me does not mind the jolt of his wagon,

The young mother and old mother comprehend me,
The girl and the wife rest the needle a moment and forget
where they are,
They and all would resume what I have told them.

## 48

I have said that the soul is not more than the body,
And I have said that the body is not more than the soul,
And nothing, not God, is greater to one than one's self is,
And whoever walks a furlong without sympathy walks to
his own funeral drest in his shroud,
And I or you pocketless of a dime may purchase the pick
of the earth,
And to glance with an eye or show a bean in its pod
confounds the learning of all times,
And there is no trade or employment but the young man
following it may become a hero,
And there is no object so soft but it makes a hub for the
wheel'd universe,
And I say to any man or woman, Let your soul stand cool
and composed before a million universes.

And I say to mankind, Be not curious about God,
For I who am curious about each am not curious about God,
(No array of terms can say how much I am at peace about
God and about death.)

I hear and behold God in every object, yet understand God
not in the least,
Nor do I understand who there can be more wonderful than
myself.

Why should I wish to see God better than this day?

I see something of God each hour of the twenty-four, and each moment then,

In the faces of men and women I see God, and in my own face in the glass,

I find letters from God dropt in the street, and every one is sign'd by God's name,

And I leave them where they are, for I know that wheresoe'er I go,

Others will punctually come for ever and ever.

## 49

And as to you Death, and you bitter hug of mortality, it is idle to try to alarm me.

To his work without flinching the accoucheur comes,
I see the elder-hand pressing receiving supporting,
I recline by the sills of the exquisite flexible doors,
And mark the outlet, and mark the relief and escape.

And as to you Corpse I think you are good manure, but that does not offend me,
I smell the white roses sweet-scented and growing,
I reach to the leafy lips, I reach to the polish'd breasts of melons.

And as to you Life I reckon you are the leavings of many deaths,
(No doubt I have died myself ten thousand times before.)

I hear you whispering there O stars of heaven,
O suns—O grass of graves—O perpetual transfers and promotions,
If you do not say any thing how can I say any thing?

Of the turbid pool that lies in the autumn forest,
Of the moon that descends the steeps of the soughing
   twilight,
Toss, sparkles of day and dusk—toss on the black stems that
   decay in the muck,
Toss to the moaning gibberish of the dry limbs.

I ascend from the moon, I ascend from the night,
I perceive that the ghastly glimmer is noonday sunbeams
   reflected,
And debouch to the steady and central from the offspring
   great or small.

## 50

There is that in me—I do not know what it is—but I know
   it is in me.

Wrench'd and sweaty—calm and cool then my body becomes,
I sleep—I sleep long.

I do not know it—it is without name—it is a word unsaid,
It is not in any dictionary, utterance, symbol.

Something it swings on more than the earth I swing on,
To it the creation is the friend whose embracing awakes me.

Perhaps I might tell more. Outlines! I plead for my brothers
   and sisters.

Do you see O my brothers and sisters?
It is not chaos or death—it is form, union, plan—it is eternal
   life—it is Happiness.

**51**

The past and present wilt—I have fill'd them, emptied
  them.
And proceed to fill my next fold of the future.

Listener up there! what have you to confide to me?
Look in my face while I snuff the sidle of evening,
(Talk honestly, no one else hears you, and I stay only a
  minute longer.)

Do I contradict myself?
Very well then I contradict myself,
(I am large, I contain multitudes.)

I concentrate toward them that are nigh, I wait on the door-
  slab.

Who has done his day's work? who will soonest be through
  with his supper?
Who wishes to walk with me?

Will you speak before I am gone? will you prove already
  too late?

**52**

The spotted hawk swoops by and accuses me, he complains
  of my gab and my loitering.

I too am not a bit tamed, I too am untranslatable,
I sound my barbaric yawp over the roofs of the world.

The last scud of day holds back for me,

It flings my likeness after the rest and true as any on the
   shadow'd wilds,
It coaxes me to the vapor and the dusk.

I depart as air, I shake my white locks at the runaway sun,
I effuse my flesh in eddies, and drift it in lacy jags.

I bequeath myself to the dirt to grow from the grass I love,
If you want me again look for me under your boot-soles.

You will hardly know who I am or what I mean,
But I shall be good health to you nevertheless,
And filter and fibre your blood.

Failing to fetch me at first keep encouraged,
Missing me one place search another,
I stop somewhere waiting for you.

# I Hear America Singing

I hear America singing, the varied carols I hear,
Those of mechanics—each one singing his as it should be
   blithe and strong,
The carpenter singing his as he measures his plank or beam,
The mason singing his as he makes ready for work, or leaves
   off work,
The boatman singing what belongs to him in his boat—the
   deck-hand singing on the steamboat deck,
The shoemaker singing as he sits on his bench—the hatter
   singing as he stands,
The wood-cutter's song—the ploughboy's on his way in the
   morning, or at noon intermission or at sundown,
The delicious singing of the mother—or of the young wife
   at work—or of the girl sewing or washing,
Each singing what belongs to him or her and to none else,
The day what belongs to the day—at night the party of
   young fellows, robust, friendly,
Singing with open mouths their strong melodious songs.

## Crossing Brooklyn Ferry

**1**

Flood-tide below me! I see you face to face!
Clouds of the west—sun there half an hour high—I see you
  also face to face.

Crowds of men and women attired in the usual costumes,
  how curious you are to me!
On the ferry-boats the hundreds and hundreds that cross,
  returning home, are more curious to me than you suppose,
And you that shall cross from shore to shore years hence
  are more to me, and more in my meditations, than you
  might suppose.

**2**

The impalpable sustenance of me from all things at all hours
  of the day,
The simple, compact, well-join'd scheme, myself disinte-
  grated, every one disintegrated yet part of the scheme,
The similitudes of the past and those of the future,
The glories strung like beads on my smallest sights and hear-
  ings, on the walk in the street and the passage over the river,
The current rushing so swiftly and swimming with me far
  away,
The others that are to follow me, the ties between me and
  them,
The certainty of others, the life, love, sight, hearing of others.

Others will enter the gates of the ferry and cross from shore
  to shore,
Others will watch the run of the flood-tide,

Others will see the shipping of Manhattan north and west,
   and the heights of Brooklyn to the south and east,
Others will see the islands large and small;
Fifty years hence, others will see them as they cross, the sun
   half an hour high,
A hundred years hence, or ever so many hundred years
   hence, others will see them,
Will enjoy the sunset, the pouring-in of the flood-tide, the
   falling-back to the sea of the ebb-tide.

### 3

It avails not, time nor place—distance avails not,
I am with you, you men and women of a generation, or
   ever so many generations hence,
Just as you feel when you look on the river and sky, so I felt,
Just as any of you is one of a living crowd, I was one of a
   crowd,
Just as you are refresh'd by the gladness of the river and the
   bright flow, I was refresh'd,
Just as you stand and lean on the rail, yet hurry with the
   swift current, I stood yet was hurried,
Just as you look on the numberless masts of ships and the
   thick-stemm'd pipes of steamboats, I look'd.

I too many and many a time cross'd the river of old,
Watched the Twelfth-month sea-gulls, saw them high in the
   air floating with motionless wings, oscillating their bodies,
Saw how the glistening yellow lit up parts of their bodies
   and left the rest in strong shadow,
Saw the slow-wheeling circles and the gradual edging toward
   the south,
Saw the reflection of the summer sky in the water,

Had my eyes dazzled by the shimmering track of beams,

Look'd at the fine centrifugal spokes of light round the shape
of my head in the sunlit water,

Look'd on the haze on the hills southward and south-
westward,

Look'd on the vapor as it flew in fleeces tinged with violet,

Look'd toward the lower bay to notice the vessels arriving,

Saw their approach, saw aboard those that were near me,

Saw the white sails of schooners and sloops, saw the ships
at anchor,

The sailors at work in the rigging or out astride the spars,

The round masts, the swinging motion of the hulls, the
slender serpentine pennants,

The large and small steamers in motion, the pilots in their
pilothouses,

The white wake left by the passage, the quick tremulous
whirl of the wheels,

The flags of all nations, the falling of them at sunset,

The scallop-edged waves in the twilight, the ladled cups,
the frolic-some crests and glistening,

The stretch afar growing dimmer and dimmer, the gray walls
of the granite storehouses by the docks,

On the river the shadowy group, the big steam-tug closely
flank'd on each side by the barges, the hay-boat, the belated
lighter,

On the neighboring shore the fires from the foundry chimneys burning high and glaringly into the night,

Casting their flicker of black contrasted with wild red and
yellow light over the tops of houses, and down into the
clefts of streets.

**4**

These and all else were to me the same as they are to you,
I loved well those cities, loved well the stately and rapid river,
The men and women I saw were all near to me,
Others the same—others who look back on me because I
   look'd forward to them,
(The time will come, though I stop here to-day and to-night.)

**5**

What is it then between us?
What is the count of the scores or hundreds of years between
   us?

Whatever it is, it avails not—distance avails not, and place
   avails not,
I too lived, Brooklyn of ample hills was mine,
I too walk'd the streets of Manhattan island, and bathed in
   the waters around it,
I too felt the curious abrupt questionings stir within me,
In the day among crowds of people sometimes they came
   upon me,
In my walks home late at night or as I lay in my bed they
   came upon me,
I too had been struck from the float forever held in solution,
I too had receiv'd identity by my body,
That I was I knew was of my body, and what I should be I
   knew I should be of my body.

**6**

It is not upon you alone the dark patches fall,
The dark threw its patches down upon me also,
The best I had done seem'd to me blank and suspicious,

My great thoughts as I supposed them, were they not in
  reality meagre?
Nor is it you alone who know what it is to be evil,
I am he who knew what it was to be evil,
I too knitted the old knot of contrariety,
Blabb'd, blush'd, resented, lied, stole, grudg'd,
Had guile, anger, lust, hot wishes I dared not speak,
Was wayward, vain, greedy, shallow, sly, cowardly, malignant,
The wolf, the snake, the hog, not wanting in me.
The cheating look, the frivolous word, the adulterous wish,
  not wanting,
Refusals, hates, postponements, meanness, laziness, none of
  these wanting,
Was one with the rest, the days and haps of the rest,
Was call'd by my nighest name by clear loud voices of young
  men as they saw me approaching or passing,
Felt their arms on my neck as I stood, or the negligent
  leaning of their flesh against me as I sat,
Saw many I loved in the street or ferry-boat or public
  assembly, yet never told them a word,
Lived the same life with the rest, the same old laughing,
  gnawing, sleeping,
Play'd the part that still looks back on the actor or actress,
The same old role, the role that is what we make it, as great
  as we like,
Or as small as we like, or both great and small.


## 7

Closer yet I approach you,
What thought you have of me now, I had as much of you—I
  laid in my stores in advance,
I consider'd long and seriously of you before you were born.

Who was to know what should come home to me?
Who knows but I am enjoying this?
Who knows, for all the distance, but I am as good as looking
at you now, for all you cannot see me?


## 8

Ah, what can ever be more stately and admirable to me than
mast-hemm'd Manhattan?
River and sunset and scallop-edg'd waves of flood-tide?
The sea-gulls oscillating their bodies, the hay-boat in the
twilight, and the belated lighter?

What gods can exceed these that clasp me by the hand, and
with voices I love call me promptly and loudly by my
nighest name as approach?
What is more subtle than this which ties me to the woman
or man that looks in my face?
Which fuses me into you now, and pours my meaning into
you?

We understand then do we not?
What I promis'd without mentioning it, have you not accepted?
What the study could not teach—what the preaching could
not accomplish is accomplish'd, is it not?


## 9

Flow on, river! flow with the flood-tide, and ebb with the
ebb-tide!
Frolic on, crested and scallop-edg'd waves!
Gorgeous clouds of the sunset! drench with your splendor
me, or the men and women generations after me!

Cross from shore to shore, countless crowds of passengers!
Stand up, tall masts of Mannahatta! stand up, beautiful hills
of Brooklyn!
Throb, baffled and curious brain! throw out questions and
answers!
Suspend here and everywhere, eternal float of solution!
Gaze, loving and thirsting eyes, in the house or street or
public assembly!


Sound out, voices of young men! loudly and musically call
me by my nighest name!
Live, old life! play the part that looks back on the actor or
actress!
Play the old role, the role that is great or small according
as one makes it!
Consider, you who peruse me, whether I may not in
unknown ways be looking upon you;
Be firm, rail over the river, to support those who lean idly,
yet haste with the hasting current;
Fly on, sea-birds! fly sideways, or wheel in large circles high
in the air;
Receive the summer sky, you water, and faithfully hold it
till all downcast eyes have time to take it from you!
Diverge, fine spokes of light, from the shape of my head,
or any one's head, in the sunlit water!
Come on, ships from the lower bay! pass up or down,
white-sail'd schooners, sloops, lighters!
Flaunt away, flags of all nations! be duly lower'd at sunset!
Burn high your fires, foundry chimneys! cast black shadows
at nightfall! cast red and yellow light over the tops of the
houses!

Appearances, now or henceforth, indicate what you are,

You necessary film, continue to envelop the soul,

About my body for me, and your body for you, be hung our divinest aromas,

Thrive, cities—bring your freight, bring your shows, ample and sufficient rivers,

Expand, being than which none else is perhaps more spiritual,

Keep your places, objects than which none else is more lasting.


You have waited, you always wait, you dumb, beautiful ministers,

We receive you with free sense at last, and are insatiate henceforward,

Not you any more shall be able to foil us, or withhold yourselves from us,

We use you, and do not cast you aside—we plant you permanently within us,

We fathom you not—we love you—there is perfection in you also,

You furnish your parts toward eternity,

Great or small, you furnish your parts toward the soul.

## Savantism

Thither as I look I see each result and glory retracing itself
 and nestling close, always obligated,
Thither hours, months, years—thither trades, compacts,
 establishments, even the most minute,
Thither every-day life, speech, utensils, politics, persons,
 estates;
Thither we also, I with my leaves and songs, trustful, admirant,
As a father to his father going takes his children along with
 him.

# Mannahatta

I was asking for something specific and perfect for my city,
Whereupon lo! upsprang the aboriginal name.

Now I see what there is in a name, a word, liquid, sane,
    unruly, musical, self-sufficient,
I see that the word of my city is that word from of old,
Because I see that word nested in nests of water-bays, superb,
Rich, hemm'd thick all around with sailships and steamships,
    an island sixteen miles long, solid-founded,
Numberless crowded streets, high growths of iron, slender,
    strong, light, splendidly uprising toward clear skies,
Tides swift and ample, well-loved by me, toward sundown,
The flowing sea-currents, the little islands, larger adjoining
    islands, the heights, the villas,
The countless masts, the white shore-steamers, the lighters,
    the ferry-boats, the black sea-steamers well-model'd,
The down-town streets, the jobbers' houses of business, the
    houses of business of the ship-merchants and money-
    brokers, the river-streets,
Immigrants arriving, fifteen or twenty thousand in a week,
The carts hauling goods, the manly race of drivers of horses,
    the brown-faced sailors,
The summer air, the bright sun shining, and the sailing
    clouds aloft,
The winter snows, the sleigh-bells, the broken ice in the river,
    passing along up or down with the flood-tide or ebb-tide,
The mechanics of the city, the masters, well-form'd, beau-
    tiful-faced, looking you straight in the eyes,
Trottoirs throng'd, vehicles, Broadway, the women, the shops
    and shows,

A million people—manners free and superb—open voices—
hospitality—the most courageous and friendly young men,
City of hurried and sparkling waters! city of spires and masts!
City nested in bays! my city!

# Out Of The Cradle Endlessly Rocking

Out of the cradle endlessly rocking,
Out of the mocking-bird's throat, the musical shuttle,
Out of the Ninth-month midnight,
Over the sterile sands and the fields beyond, where the child leaving his bed wander'd alone, bareheaded, barefoot,
Down from the shower'd halo,
Up from the mystic play of shadows twining and twisting as if they were alive,
Out from the patches of briers and blackberries,
From the memories of the bird that chanted to me,
From your memories sad brother, from the fitful risings and fallings I heard,
From under that yellow half-moon late-risen and swollen as if with tears,
From those beginning notes of yearning and love there in the mist,
From the thousand responses of my heart never to cease,
From the myriad thence-arous'd words,
From the word stronger and more delicious than any,
From such as now they start the scene revisiting,
As a flock, twittering, rising, or overhead passing,
Borne hither, ere all eludes me, hurriedly,
A man, yet by these tears a little boy again,
Throwing myself on the sand, confronting the waves,
I, chanter of pains and joys, uniter of here and hereafter,
Taking all hints to use them, but swiftly leaping beyond them,
A reminiscence sing.

Once Paumanok,
When the lilac-scent was in the air and Fifth-month grass
  was growing,
Up this seashore in some briers,
Two feather'd guests from Alabama, two together,
And their nest, and four light-green eggs spotted with brown,
And every day the he-bird to and fro near at hand,
And every day the she-bird crouch'd on her nest, silent, with
  bright eyes,
And every day I, a curious boy, never too close, never
  disturbing them,
Cautiously peering, absorbing, translating.

*Shine! shine! shine!*
*Pour down your warmth, great sun!*
*While we bask, we two together.*

*Two together!*
*Winds blow south, or winds blow north,*
*Day come white, or night come black,*
*Home, or rivers and mountains from home,*
*Singing all time, minding no time,*
*While we two keep together.*

Till of a sudden,
May-be kill'd, unknown to her mate,
One forenoon the she-bird crouch'd not on the nest,
Nor return'd that afternoon, nor the next,
Nor ever appear'd again.

And thenceforward all summer in the sound of the sea,
And at night under the full of the moon in calmer weather,

Over the hoarse surging of the sea,
Or flitting from brier to brier by day,
I saw, I heard at intervals the remaining one, the he-bird,
The solitary guest from Alabama.

*Blow! blow! blow!*
*Blow up sea-winds along Paumanok's shore;*
*I wait and I wait till you blow my mate to me.*

Yes, when the stars glisten'd,
All night long on the prong of a moss-scallop'd stake,
Down almost amid the slapping waves,
Sat the lone singer wonderful causing tears.

He call'd on his mate,
He pour'd forth the meanings which I of all men know.

Yes my brother I know,
The rest might not, but I have treasur'd every note,
For more than once dimly down to the beach gliding,
Silent, avoiding the moonbeams, blending myself with the
    shadows,
Recalling now the obscure shapes, the echoes, the sounds
    and sights after their sorts,
The white arms out in the breakers tirelessly tossing,
I, with bare feet, a child, the wind wafting my hair,
Listen'd long and long.

Listen'd to keep, to sing, now translating the notes,
Following you my brother.

Soothe! soothe! soothe!
Close on its wave soothes the wave behind,
And again another behind embracing and lapping, every one close,
But my love soothes not me, not me.

Low hangs the moon, it rose late,
It is lagging—O I think it is heavy with love, with love.

O madly the sea pushes upon the land,
With love, with love.

O night! do I not see my love fluttering out among the breakers?
What is that little black thing I see there in the white?

Loud! loud! loud!
Loud I call to you, my love!
High and clear I shoot my voice over the waves,
Surely you must know who is here, is here,
You must know who I am, my love.

Low-hanging moon!
What is that dusky spot in your brown yellow?
O it is the shape, the shape of my mate!
O moon do not keep her from me any longer.

Land! land! O land!
Whichever way I turn, O I think you could give me my mate back again
     if you only would,
For I am almost sure I see her dimly whichever way I look.

O rising stars!
Perhaps the one I want so much will rise, will rise with some of you.

O throat! O trembling throat!
Sound clearer through the atmosphere!
Pierce the woods, the earth,
Somewhere listening to catch you must be the one I want.

Shake out carols!
Solitary here, the night's carols!
Carols of lonesome love! death's carols!
Carols under that lagging, yellow, waning moon!
O under that moon where she droops almost down into the sea!
O reckless despairing carols.

But soft! sink low!
Soft! let me just murmur,
And do you wait a moment you husky-nois'd sea,
For somewhere I believe I heard my mate responding to me,
So faint, I must be still, be still to listen,
But not altogether still, for then she might not come immediately to me.

Hither my love!
Here I am! here!
With this just-sustain'd note I announce myself to you,
This gentle call is for you my love, for you.

Do not be decoy'd elsewhere,
That is the whistle of the wind, it is not my voice,
That is the fluttering, the fluttering of the spray,
Those are the shadows of leaves.

O darkness! O in vain!
O I am very sick and sorrowful.

O brown halo in the sky near the moon, drooping upon the sea!
O troubled reflection in the sea!
O throat! O throbbing heart!
And I singing uselessly, uselessly all the night.

O past! O happy life! O songs of joy!
In the air, in the woods, over fields,
Loved! loved! loved! loved! loved!
But my mate no more, no more with me!
We two together no more.

The aria sinking,
All else continuing, the stars shining,
The winds blowing, the notes of the bird continuous echoing,
With angry moans the fierce old mother incessantly moaning,
On the sands of Paumanok's shore gray and rustling,
The yellow half-moon enlarged, sagging down, drooping, the face of the sea almost touching,
The boy ecstatic, with his bare feet the waves, with his hair the atmosphere dallying,
The love in the heart long pent, now loose, now at last tumultuously bursting,
The aria's meaning, the ears, the soul, swiftly depositing,
The strange tears down the cheeks coursing,
The colloquy there, the trio, each uttering,
The undertone, the savage old mother incessantly crying,
To the boy's soul's questions sullenly timing, some drown'd secret hissing,
To the outsetting bard.

Demon or bird! (said the boy's soul,)

Is it indeed toward your mate you sing? or is it really to me?

For I, that was a child, my tongue's use sleeping, now I have
heard you,

Now in a moment I know what I am for, I awake,

And already a thousand singers, a thousand songs, clearer,
louder and more sorrowful than yours,

A thousand warbling echoes have started to life within me,
never to die.

O you singer solitary, singing by yourself, projecting me,

O solitary me listening, never more shall I cease perpetuating
you,

Never more shall I escape, never more the reverberations,

Never more the cries of unsatisfied love be absent from me,

Never again leave me to be the peaceful child I was before
what there in the night,

By the sea under the yellow and sagging moon,

The messenger there arous'd, the fire, the sweet hell within,

The unknown want, the destiny of me.


O give me the clew! (it lurks in the night here somewhere,)

O if I am to have so much, let me have more!


A word then, (for I will conquer it,)

The word final, superior to all,

Subtle, sent up—what is it?—I listen;

Are you whispering it, and have been all the time, you sea-
waves?

Is that it from your liquid rims and wet sands?


Whereto answering, the sea,

Delaying not, hurrying not,

Whisper'd me through the night, and very plainly before
   day-break,
Lisp'd to me the low and delicious word death,
And again death, death, death, death,
Hissing melodious, neither like the bird nor like my arous'd
   child's heart,
But edging near as privately for me rustling at my feet,
Creeping thence steadily up to my ears and laving me softly
   all over,
Death, death, death, death, death.

Which I do not forget,
But fuse the song of my dusky demon and brother,
That he sang to me in the moonlight on Paumanok's gray
   beach,
With the thousand responsive songs at random,
My own songs awaked from that hour,
And with them the key, the word up from the waves,
The word of the sweetest song and all songs,
That strong and delicious word which, creeping to my feet,
(Or like some old crone rocking the cradle, swathed in sweet
   garments, bending aside,)
The sea whisper'd me.

## I Saw In Louisiana A Live-Oak Growing

I saw in Louisiana a live-oak growing,
All alone stood it and the moss hung down from the
    branches,
Without any companion it grew there uttering joyous leaves
    of dark green,
And its look, rude, unbending, lusty, made me think of
    myself,
But I wonder'd how it could utter joyous leaves standing
    alone there without its friend near, for I knew I could not,
And I broke off a twig with a certain number of leaves upon
    it, and twined around it a little moss,
And brought it away, and I have placed it in sight in my
    room,
It is not needed to remind me as of my own dear friends,
(For I believe lately I think of little else than of them,)
Yet it remains to me a curious token, it makes me think of
    manly love;
For all that, and though the live-oak glistens there in
    Louisiana solitary in a wide flat space,
Uttering joyous leaves all its life without a friend a lover
    near,
I know very well I could not.

# Whoever You Are Holding Me Now In Hand

Whoever you are holding me now in hand,
Without one thing all will be useless,
I give you fair warning before you attempt me further,
I am not what you supposed, but far different.

Who is he that would become my follower?
Who would sign himself a candidate for my affections?

The way is suspicious, the result uncertain, perhaps destruc-
  tive,
You would have to give up all else, I alone would expect to
  be your sole and exclusive standard,
Your novitiate would even then be long and exhausting,
The whole past theory of your life and all conformity to
  the lives around you would have to be abandon'd,
Therefore release me now before troubling yourself any
  further, let go your hand from my shoulders,
Put me down and depart on your way.

Or else by stealth in some wood for trial,
Or back of a rock in the open air,
(For in any roof'd room of a house I emerge not, nor in
  company,
And in libraries I lie as one dumb, a gawk, or unborn, or
  dead,)
But just possibly with you on a high hill, first watching lest
  any person for miles around approach unawares,
Or possibly with you sailing at sea, or on the beach of the
  sea or some quiet island,
Here to put your lips upon mine I permit you,

With the comrade's long-dwelling kiss or the new husband's
     kiss,
For I am the new husband and I am the comrade.

Or if you will, thrusting me beneath your clothing,
Where I may feel the throbs of your heart or rest upon your
     hip,
Carry me when you go forth over land or sea;
For thus merely touching you is enough, is best,
And thus touching you would I silently sleep and be carried
     eternally.

But these leaves conning you con at peril,
For these leaves and me you will not understand,
They will elude you at first and still more afterward, I will
     certainly elude you,
Even while you should think you had unquestionably caught
     me, behold!
Already you see I have escaped from you.

For it is not for what I have put into it that I have written
     this book,
Nor is it by reading it you will acquire it,
Nor do those know me best who admire me and vauntingly
     praise me,
Nor will the candidates for my love (unless at most a very
     few) prove victorious,
Nor will my poems do good only, they will do just as much
     evil, perhaps more,
For all is useless without that which you may guess at many
     times and not hit, that which I hinted at;
Therefore release me and depart on your way.

## One Hour To Madness And Joy

One hour to madness and joy! O furious! O confine me
    not!
(What is this that frees me so in storms?
What do my shouts amid lightnings and raging winds mean?)

O to drink the mystic deliria deeper than any other man!
O savage and tender achings! (I bequeath them to you my
    children,
I tell them to you, for reasons, O bridegroom and bride.)

O to be yielded to you whoever you are, and you to be
    yielded to me in defiance of the world!
O to return to Paradise! O bashful and feminine!
O to draw you to me, to plant on you for the first time the
    lips of a determin'd man.

O the puzzle, the thrice-tied knot, the deep and dark pool,
    all untied and illumin'd!
O to speed where there is space enough and air enough at
    last!
To be absolv'd from previous ties and conventions, I from
    mine and you from yours!
To find a new unthought-of nonchalance with the best of
    Nature!
To have the gag remov'd from one's mouth!
To have the feeling to-day or any day I am sufficient as I
    am.

O something unprov'd! something in a trance!
To escape utterly from others' anchors and holds!

To drive free! to love free! to dash reckless and dangerous!
To court destruction with taunts, with invitations!
To ascend, to leap to the heavens of the love indicated to
  me!
To rise thither with my inebriate soul!
To be lost if it must be so!
To feed the remainder of life with one hour of fulness and
  freedom!
With one brief hour of madness and joy.

## Beat! Beat! Drums!

Beat! beat! drums!—blow! bugles! blow!
Through the windows—through doors—burst like a ruthless
  force,
Into the solemn church, and scatter the congregation,
Into the school where the scholar is studying;
Leave not the bridegroom quiet—no happiness must he have
  now with his bride,
Nor the peaceful farmer any peace, ploughing his field or
  gathering his grain,
So fierce you whirr and pound you drums—so shrill you
  bugles blow.

Beat! beat! drums!—blow! bugles! blow!
Over the traffic of cities—over the rumble of wheels in the
  streets;
Are beds prepared for sleepers at night in the houses? no
  sleepers must sleep in those beds,
No bargainers' bargains by day—no brokers or speculators—
would they continue?
Would the talkers be talking? would the singer attempt to
  sing?
Would the lawyer rise in the court to state his case before
  the judge?
Then rattle quicker, heavier drums—you bugles wilder blow.

Beat! beat! drums!—blow! bugles! blow!
Make no parley—stop for no expostulation,
Mind not the timid—mind not the weeper or prayer,
Mind not the old man beseeching the young man,
Let not the child's voice be heard, nor the mother's entreaties,

Make even the trestles to shake the dead where they lie
  awaiting the hearses,
So strong you thump O terrible drums—so loud you bugles
  blow.

## To One Shortly To Die

From all the rest I single out you, having a message for you,
You are to die—let others tell you what they please, I cannot
   prevaricate,
I am exact and merciless, but I love you—there is no escape
   for you.

Softly I lay my right hand upon you, you just feel it,
I do not argue, I bend my head close and half envelop it,
I sit quietly by, I remain faithful,
I am more than nurse, more than parent or neighbor,
I absolve you from all except yourself spiritual bodily, that
   is eternal, you yourself will surely escape,
The corpse you will leave will be but excrementitious.

The sun bursts through in unlooked-for directions,
Strong thoughts fill you and confidence, you smile,
You forget you are sick, as I forget you are sick,
You do not see the medicines, you do not mind the weeping
   friends, I am with you,
I exclude others from you, there is nothing to be commis-
   erated,
I do not commiserate, I congratulate you.

# Vigil Strange I Kept On The Field One Night

Vigil strange I kept on the field one night;

When you my son and my comrade dropt at my side that day,

One look I but gave which your dear eyes return'd with a look I shall never forget,

One touch of your hand to mine O boy, reach'd up as you lay on the ground,

Then onward I sped in the battle, the even-contested battle,

Till late in the night reliev'd to the place at last again I made my way,

Found you in death so cold dear comrade, found your body son of responding kisses, (never again on earth responding,)

Bared your face in the starlight, curious the scene, cool blew the moderate night-wind,

Long there and then in vigil I stood, dimly around me the battle-field spreading,

Vigil wondrous and vigil sweet there in the fragrant silent night,

But not a tear fell, not even a long-drawn sigh, long, long I gazed,

Then on the earth partially reclining sat by your side leaning my chin in my hands,

Passing sweet hours, immortal and mystic hours with you dearest comrade—not a tear, not a word,

Vigil of silence, love and death, vigil for you my son and my soldier,

As onward silently stars aloft, eastward new ones upward stole,

Vigil final for you brave boy, (I could not save you, swift was your death,

I faithfully loved you and cared for you living, I think we
   shall surely meet again,)
Till at latest lingering of the night, indeed just as the dawn
   appear'd,
My comrade I wrapt in his blanket, envelop'd well his form,
Folded the blanket well, tucking it carefully over head and
   carefully under feet,
And there and then and bathed by the rising sun, my son
   in his grave, in his rude-dug grave I deposited,
Ending my vigil strange with that, vigil of night and battle-
   field dim,
Vigil for boy of responding kisses, (never again on earth
   responding,)
Vigil for comrade swiftly slain, vigil I never forget, how as
   day brighten'd,
I rose from the chill ground and folded my soldier well in
   his blanket,
And buried him where he fell.

## I Sing The Body Electric

**1**

I sing the body electric,
The armies of those I love engirth me and I engirth them,
They will not let me off till I go with them, respond to them,
And discorrupt them, and charge them full with the charge
of the soul.
Was it doubted that those who corrupt their own bodies
conceal themselves?
And if those who defile the living are as bad as they who
defile the dead?
And if the body does not do fully as much as the soul?
And if the body were not the soul, what is the soul?

**2**

The love of the body of man or woman balks account, the
body itself balks account,
That of the male is perfect, and that of the female is perfect.
The expression of the face balks account,
But the expression of a well-made man appears not only in
his face,
It is in his limbs and joints also, it is curiously in the joints
of his hips and wrists,
It is in his walk, the carriage of his neck, the flex of his
waist and knees, dress does not hide him,
The strong sweet quality he has strikes through the cotton
and broadcloth,
To see him pass conveys as much as the best poem, perhaps
more,
You linger to see his back, and the back of his neck and
shoulder-side.

The sprawl and fulness of babes, the bosoms and heads of women, the folds of their dress, their style as we pass in the street, the contour of their shape downwards,

The swimmer naked in the swimming-bath, seen as he swims through the transparent green-shine, or lies with his face up and rolls silently to and fro in the heave of the water,

The bending forward and backward of rowers in row-boats, the horseman in his saddle,

Girls, mothers, house-keepers, in all their performances,

The group of laborers seated at noon-time with their open dinner-kettles, and their wives waiting,

The female soothing a child, the farmer's daughter in the garden or cow-yard,

The young fellow hoeing corn, the sleigh-driver driving his six horses through the crowd,

The wrestle of wrestlers, two apprentice-boys, quite grown, lusty, good-natured, native-born, out on the vacant lot at sun-down after work,

The coats and caps thrown down, the embrace of love and resistance,

The upper-hold and under-hold, the hair rumpled over and blinding the eyes;

The march of firemen in their own costumes, the play of masculine muscle through clean-setting trowsers and waist-straps,

The slow return from the fire, the pause when the bell strikes suddenly again, and the listening on the alert,

The natural, perfect, varied attitudes, the bent head, the curv'd neck and the counting;

Such-like I love—I loosen myself, pass freely, am at the mother's breast with the little child,

Swim with the swimmers, wrestle with wrestlers, march in
line with the firemen, and pause, listen, count.

**3**

I knew a man, a common farmer, the father of five sons,
And in them the fathers of sons, and in them the fathers of
sons.

This man was of wonderful vigor, calmness, beauty of person,
The shape of his head, the pale yellow and white of his hair
and beard, the immeasurable meaning of his black eyes,
the richness and breadth of his manners,
These I used to go and visit him to see, he was wise also,
He was six feet tall, he was over eighty years old, his sons
were massive, clean, bearded, tan-faced, handsome,
They and his daughters loved him, all who saw him loved
him,
They did not love him by allowance, they loved him with
personal love,
He drank water only, the blood show'd like scarlet through
the clear-brown skin of his face,
He was a frequent gunner and fisher, he sail'd his boat himself,
he had a fine one presented to him by a ship-joiner, he had
fowling-pieces presented to him by men that loved him,
When he went with his five sons and many grand-sons to
hunt or fish, you would pick him out as the most beautiful
and vigorous of the gang,
You would wish long and long to be with him, you would
wish to sit by him in the boat that you and he might
touch each other.

**4**

I have perceiv'd that to be with those I like is enough,
To stop in company with the rest at evening is enough,
To be surrounded by beautiful, curious, breathing, laughing
  flesh is enough,
To pass among them or touch any one, or rest my arm ever
  so lightly round his or her neck for a moment, what is
  this then?
I do not ask any more delight, I swim in it as in a sea.


There is something in staying close to men and women and
  looking on them, and in the contact and odor of them,
  that pleases the soul well,
All things please the soul, but these please the soul well.


**5**

This is the female form,
A divine nimbus exhales from it from head to foot,
It attracts with fierce undeniable attraction,
I am drawn by its breath as if I were no more than a help-
  less vapor, all falls aside but myself and it,
Books, art, religion, time, the visible and solid earth, and what
  was expected of heaven or fear'd of hell, are now consumed,
Mad filaments, ungovernable shoots play out of it, the
  response likewise ungovernable,
Hair, bosom, hips, bend of legs, negligent falling hands all
  diffused, mine too diffused,
Ebb stung by the flow and flow stung by the ebb, love-flesh
  swelling and deliciously aching,
Limitless limpid jets of love hot and enormous, quivering
  jelly of love, white-blow and delirious juice,

Bridegroom night of love working surely and softly into the
prostrate dawn,
Undulating into the willing and yielding day,
Lost in the cleave of the clasping and sweet-flesh'd day.

This the nucleus—after the child is born of woman, man
is born of woman,
This the bath of birth, this the merge of small and large,
and the outlet again.

Be not ashamed women, your privilege encloses the rest,
and is the exit of the rest,
You are the gates of the body, and you are the gates of the
soul.

The female contains all qualities and tempers them,
She is in her place and moves with perfect balance,
She is all things duly veil'd, she is both passive and active,
She is to conceive daughters as well as sons, and sons as
well as daughters.

As I see my soul reflected in Nature,
As I see through a mist, One with inexpressible completeness,
sanity, beauty,
See the bent head and arms folded over the breast, the Female
I see.

6

The male is not less the soul nor more, he too is in his
place,
He too is all qualities, he is action and power,
The flush of the known universe is in him,

Scorn becomes him well, and appetite and defiance become
  him well,
The wildest largest passions, bliss that is utmost, sorrow that
  is utmost become him well, pride is for him,
The full-spread pride of man is calming and excellent to the
  soul,
Knowledge becomes him, he likes it always, he brings every
  thing to the test of himself,
Whatever the survey, whatever the sea and the sail he strikes
  soundings at last only here,
(Where else does he strike soundings except here?)

The man's body is sacred and the woman's body is sacred,
No matter who it is, it is sacred—is it the meanest one in
  the laborers' gang?
Is it one of the dull-faced immigrants just landed on the wharf?
Each belongs here or anywhere just as much as the well-off,
  just as much as you,
Each has his or her place in the procession.

(All is a procession,
The universe is a procession with measured and perfect motion.)

Do you know so much yourself that you call the meanest
  ignorant?
Do you suppose you have a right to a good sight, and he
  or she has no right to a sight?
Do you think matter has cohered together from its diffuse
  float, and the soil is on the surface, and water runs and
  vegetation sprouts,
For you only, and not for him and her?

**7**

A man's body at auction,
(For before the war I often go to the slave-mart and watch
  the sale,)
I help the auctioneer, the sloven does not half know his
  business.

Gentlemen look on this wonder,
Whatever the bids of the bidders they cannot be high enough
  for it,
For it the globe lay preparing quintillions of years without
  one animal or plant,
For it the revolving cycles truly and steadily roll'd.

In this head the all-baffling brain,
In it and below it the makings of heroes.

Examine these limbs, red, black, or white, they are cunning
  in tendon and nerve,
They shall be stript that you may see them.

Exquisite senses, life-lit eyes, pluck, volition,
Flakes of breast-muscle, pliant backbone and neck, flesh not
  flabby, good-sized arms and legs,
And wonders within there yet.

Within there runs blood,
The same old blood! the same red-running blood!
There swells and jets a heart, there all passions, desires,
  reachings, aspirations,
(Do you think they are not there because they are not
  express'd in parlors and lecture-rooms?)

This is not only one man, this the father of those who shall
 be fathers in their turns,
In him the start of populous states and rich republics,
Of him countless immortal lives with countless embodiments
 and enjoyments.

How do you know who shall come from the offspring of
 his off-spring through the centuries?
(Who might you find you have come from yourself, if you
 could trace back through the centuries?)

**8**
A woman's body at auction,
She too is not only herself, she is the teeming mother of mothers,
She is the bearer of them that shall grow and be mates to
 the mothers.

Have you ever loved the body of a woman?
Have you ever loved the body of a man?
Do you not see that these are exactly the same to all in all
 nations and times all over the earth?

If any thing is sacred the human body is sacred,
And the glory and sweet of a man is the token of manhood
 untainted,
And in man or woman a clean, strong, firm-fibred body, is
 more beautiful than the most beautiful face.

Have you seen the fool that corrupted his own live body?
 or the fool that corrupted her own live body?
For they do not conceal themselves, and cannot conceal
 themselves.

## 9

O my body! I dare not desert the likes of you in other men
 and women, nor the likes of the parts of you,
I believe the likes of you are to stand or fall with the likes
 of the soul, (and that they are the soul,)
I believe the likes of you shall stand or fall with my poems,
 and that they are my poems,
Man's, woman's, child's, youth's, wife's, husband's, mother's,
 father's, young man's, young woman's poems,
Head, neck, hair, ears, drop and tympan of the ears,
Eyes, eye-fringes, iris of the eye, eyebrows, and the waking
 or sleeping of the lids,
Mouth, tongue, lips, teeth, roof of the mouth, jaws, and the
 jaw-hinges,
Nose, nostrils of the nose, and the partition,
Cheeks, temples, forehead, chin, throat, back of the neck,
 neck-slue,
Strong shoulders, manly beard, scapula, hind-shoulders, and
 the ample side-round of the chest,
Upper-arm, armpit, elbow-socket, lower-arm, arm-sinews,
 arm-bones,
Wrist and wrist-joints, hand, palm, knuckles, thumb, fore-
 finger, finger-joints, finger-nails,
Broad breast-front, curling hair of the breast, breast-bone,
 breast-side,
Ribs, belly, backbone, joints of the backbone,
Hips, hip-sockets, hip-strength, inward and outward round,
 man-balls, man-root,
Strong set of thighs, well carrying the trunk above,
Leg-fibres, knee, knee-pan, upper-leg, under-leg,
Ankles, instep, foot-ball, toes, toe-joints, the heel;

All attitudes, all the shapeliness, all the belongings of my or
    your body or of any one's body, male or female,
The lung-sponges, the stomach-sac, the bowels sweet and clean,
The brain in its folds inside the skull-frame,
Sympathies, heart-valves, palate-valves, sexuality, maternity,
Womanhood, and all that is a woman, and the man that
    comes from woman,
The womb, the teats, nipples, breast-milk, tears, laughter,
    weeping, love-looks, love-perturbations and risings,
The voice, articulation, language, whispering, shouting aloud,
Food, drink, pulse, digestion, sweat, sleep, walking, swimming,
Poise on the hips, leaping, reclining, embracing, arm-curving
    and tightening,
The continual changes of the flex of the mouth, and around
    the eyes,
The skin, the sunburnt shade, freckles, hair,
The curious sympathy one feels when feeling with the hand
    the naked meat of the body,
The circling rivers the breath, and breathing it in and out,
The beauty of the waist, and thence of the hips, and thence
    downward toward the knees,
The thin red jellies within you or within me, the bones and
    the marrow in the bones,
The exquisite realization of health;
O I say these are not the parts and poems of the body only,
    but of the soul,
O I say now these are the soul!

## Pioneers! O Pioneers!

Come my tan-faced children,
Follow well in order, get your weapons ready,
Have you your pistols? have you your sharp-edged axes?
Pioneers! O pioneers!

For we cannot tarry here,
We must march my darlings, we must bear the brunt of
    danger,
We the youthful sinewy races, all the rest on us depend,
Pioneers! O pioneers!

O you youths, Western youths,
So impatient, full of action, full of manly pride and friend-
    ship,
Plain I see you Western youths, see you tramping with the
    foremost,
Pioneers! O pioneers!

Have the elder races halted?
Do they droop and end their lesson, wearied over there
    beyond the seas?
We take up the task eternal, and the burden and the lesson,
Pioneers! O pioneers!

All the past we leave behind,
We debouch upon a newer mightier world, varied world,
Fresh and strong the world we seize, world of labor and the
    march,
Pioneers! O pioneers!

We detachments steady throwing,
Down the edges, through the passes, up the mountains steep,
Conquering, holding, daring, venturing as we go the
 unknown ways,
Pioneers! O pioneers!

We primeval forests felling,
We the rivers stemming, vexing we and piercing deep the
 mines within,
We the surface broad surveying, we the virgin soil upheaving,
Pioneers! O pioneers!

Colorado men are we,
From the peaks gigantic, from the great sierras and the high
 plateaus,
From the mine and from the gully, from the hunting trail
 we come,
Pioneers! O pioneers!
From Nebraska, from Arkansas,
Central inland race are we, from Missouri, with the conti-
 nental blood intervein'd,
All the hands of comrades clasping, all the Southern, all the
 Northern,
Pioneers! O pioneers!

O resistless restless race!
O beloved race in all! O my breast aches with tender love
 for all!
O I mourn and yet exult, I am rapt with love for all,
Pioneers! O pioneers!

Raise the mighty mother mistress,

Waving high the delicate mistress, over all the starry mistress,
(bend your heads all,)
Raise the fang'd and warlike mistress, stern, impassive, weap-
on'd mistress,
Pioneers! O pioneers!

See my children, resolute children,
By those swarms upon our rear we must never yield or
falter,
Ages back in ghostly millions frowning there behind us
urging,
Pioneers! O pioneers!

On and on the compact ranks,
With accessions ever waiting, with the places of the dead
quickly fill'd,
Through the battle, through defeat, moving yet and never
stopping,
Pioneers! O pioneers!

O to die advancing on!
Are there some of us to droop and die? has the hour come?
Then upon the march we fittest die, soon and sure the gap
is fill'd,
Pioneers! O pioneers!

All the pulses of the world,
Falling in they beat for us, with the Western movement beat,
Holding single or together, steady moving to the front, all
for us,
Pioneers! O pioneers!

Life's involv'd and varied pageants,
All the forms and shows, all the workmen at their work,
All the seamen and the landsmen, all the masters with their
  slaves,
Pioneers! O pioneers!

All the hapless silent lovers,
All the prisoners in the prisons, all the righteous and the
  wicked,
All the joyous, all the sorrowing, all the living, all the dying,
Pioneers! O pioneers!

I too with my soul and body,
We, a curious trio, picking, wandering on our way,
Through these shores amid the shadows, with the apparitions
  pressing,
Pioneers! O pioneers!

Lo, the darting bowling orb!
Lo, the brother orbs around, all the clustering suns and
  planets,
All the dazzling days, all the mystic nights with dreams,
Pioneers! O pioneers!

These are of us, they are with us,
All for primal needed work, while the followers there in
  embryo wait behind,
We to-day's procession heading, we the route for travel
  clearing,
Pioneers! O pioneers!

O you daughters of the West!

O you young and elder daughters! O you mothers and you
  wives!
Never must you be divided, in our ranks you move united,
Pioneers! O pioneers!

Minstrels latent on the prairies!
(Shrouded bards of other lands, you may rest, you have done
  your work,)
Soon I hear you coming warbling, soon you rise and tramp
  amid us,
Pioneers! O pioneers!

Not for delectations sweet,
Not the cushion and the slipper, not the peaceful and the
  studious,
Not the riches safe and palling, not for us the tame enjoy-
  ment,
Pioneers! O pioneers!

Do the feasters gluttonous feast?
Do the corpulent sleepers sleep? have they lock'd and bolted
  doors?
Still be ours the diet hard, and the blanket on the ground,
Pioneers! O pioneers!
Has the night descended?
Was the road of late so toilsome? did we stop discouraged
  nodding on our way?
Yet a passing hour I yield you in your tracks to pause obliv-
  ious,
Pioneers! O pioneers!

Till with sound of trumpet,
Far, far off the daybreak call—hark! how loud and clear I
hear it wind,
Swift! to the head of the army!—swift! spring to your places,
Pioneers! O pioneers!

# The Wound-Dresser

## 1

An old man bending I come among new faces,

Years looking backward resuming in answer to children,

Come tell us old man, as from young men and maidens that
love me,

(Arous'd and angry, I'd thought to beat the alarum, and urge
relentless war,

But soon my fingers fail'd me, my face droop'd and I resign'd
myself,

To sit by the wounded and soothe them, or silently watch
the dead;)

Years hence of these scenes, of these furious passions, these
chances,

Of unsurpass'd heroes, (was one side so brave? the other
was equally brave;)

Now be witness again, paint the mightiest armies of earth,

Of those armies so rapid so wondrous what saw you to tell us?

What stays with you latest and deepest? of curious panics,

Of hard-fought engagements or sieges tremendous what
deepest remains?

## 2

O maidens and young men I love and that love me,

What you ask of my days those the strangest and sudden
your talking recalls,

Soldier alert I arrive after a long march cover'd with sweat
and dust,

In the nick of time I come, plunge in the fight, loudly shout
in the rush of successful charge,

Enter the captur'd works—yet lo, like a swift-running river
    they fade,
Pass and are gone they fade—I dwell not on soldiers' perils
    or soldiers' joys,
(Both I remember well—many the hardships, few the joys,
    yet I was content.)

But in silence, in dreams' projections,
While the world of gain and appearance and mirth goes on,
So soon what is over forgotten, and waves wash the imprints
    off the sand,
With hinged knees returning I enter the doors, (while for
    you up there,
Whoever you are, follow without noise and be of strong
    heart.)

Bearing the bandages, water and sponge,
Straight and swift to my wounded I go,
Where they lie on the ground after the battle brought in,
Where their priceless blood reddens the grass the ground,
Or to the rows of the hospital tent, or under the roof'd
    hospital,
To the long rows of cots up and down each side I return,
To each and all one after another I draw near, not one do I
    miss,
An attendant follows holding a tray, he carries a refuse pail,
Soon to be fill'd with clotted rags and blood, emptied, and
    fill'd again.

I onward go, I stop,
With hinged knees and steady hand to dress wounds,

I am firm with each, the pangs are sharp yet unavoidable,
One turns to me his appealing eyes—poor boy! I never knew
you,
Yet I think I could not refuse this moment to die for you,
if that would save you.


**3**
On, on I go, (open doors of time! open hospital doors!)
The crush'd head I dress, (poor crazed hand tear not the
bandage away,)
The neck of the cavalry-man with the bullet through and
through I examine,
Hard the breathing rattles, quite glazed already the eye, yet
life struggles hard,
(Come sweet death! be persuaded O beautiful death!
In mercy come quickly.)

From the stump of the arm, the amputated hand,
I undo the clotted lint, remove the slough, wash off the
matter and blood,
Back on his pillow the soldier bends with curv'd neck and
side-falling head,
His eyes are closed, his face is pale, he dares not look on
the bloody stump,
And has not yet look'd on it.

I dress a wound in the side, deep, deep,
But a day or two more, for see the frame all wasted and sinking,
And the yellow-blue countenance see.

I dress the perforated shoulder, the foot with the bullet-
wound,

Cleanse the one with a gnawing and putrid gangrene, so
    sickening, so offensive,
While the attendant stands behind aside me holding the tray
    and pail.

I am faithful, I do not give out,
The fractur'd thigh, the knee, the wound in the abdomen,
These and more I dress with impassive hand, (yet deep in
    my breast a fire, a burning flame.)

**4**
Thus in silence in dreams' projections,
Returning, resuming, I thread my way through the hospitals,
The hurt and wounded I pacify with soothing hand,
I sit by the restless all the dark night, some are so young,

Some suffer so much, I recall the experience sweet and sad,
(Many a soldier's loving arms about this neck have cross'd
    and rested,
Many a soldier's kiss dwells on these bearded lips.)

# When Lilacs Last In The Dooryard Bloom'd

**1**

When lilacs last in the dooryard bloom'd,
And the great star early droop'd in the western sky in the
 night,
I mourn'd, and yet shall mourn with ever-returning spring.

Ever-returning spring, trinity sure to me you bring,
Lilac blooming perennial and drooping star in the west,
And thought of him I love.

**2**

O powerful western fallen star!
O shades of night—O moody, tearful night!
O great star disappear'd—O the black murk that hides the star!
O cruel hands that hold me powerless—O helpless soul of
 me!
O harsh surrounding cloud that will not free my soul.

**3**

In the dooryard fronting an old farm-house near the whitewash'd palings,
Stands the lilac-bush tall-growing with heart-shaped leaves
 of rich green,
With many a pointed blossom rising delicate, with the
 perfume strong I love,
With every leaf a miracle—and from this bush in the dooryard,
With delicate-color'd blossoms and heart-shaped leaves of
 rich green,
A sprig with its flower I break.

**4**

In the swamp in secluded recesses,
A shy and hidden bird is warbling a song.

Solitary the thrush,
The hermit withdrawn to himself, avoiding the settlements,
Sings by himself a song.

Song of the bleeding throat,
Death's outlet song of life, (for well dear brother I know,
If thou wast not granted to sing thou would'st surely
    die.)

**5**

Over the breast of the spring, the land, amid cities,
Amid lanes and through old woods, where lately the violets
    peep'd from the ground, spotting the gray debris,
Amid the grass in the fields each side of the lanes, passing
    the endless grass,
Passing the yellow-spear'd wheat, every grain from its shroud
    in the dark-brown fields uprisen,
Passing the apple-tree blows of white and pink in the
    orchards,
Carrying a corpse to where it shall rest in the grave,
Night and day journeys a coffin.

**6**

Coffin that passes through lanes and streets,
Through day and night with the great cloud darkening the
    land,
With the pomp of the inloop'd flags with the cities draped
    in black,

With the show of the States themselves as of crape-veil'd
   women standing,
With processions long and winding and the flambeaus of
   the night,
With the countless torches lit, with the silent sea of faces
   and the unbared heads,
With the waiting depot, the arriving coffin, and the sombre
   faces,
With dirges through the night, with the thousand voices
   rising strong and solemn,
With all the mournful voices of the dirges pour'd around
   the coffin,
The dim-lit churches and the shuddering organs—where
   amid these you journey,
With the tolling tolling bells' perpetual clang,
Here, coffin that slowly passes,
I give you my sprig of lilac.

### 7

(Nor for you, for one alone,
Blossoms and branches green to coffins all I bring,
For fresh as the morning, thus would I chant a song for you
   O sane and sacred death.

All over bouquets of roses,
O death, I cover you over with roses and early lilies,
But mostly and now the lilac that blooms the first,
Copious I break, I break the sprigs from the bushes,
With loaded arms I come, pouring for you,
For you and the coffins all of you O death.)

**8**

O western orb sailing the heaven,

Now I know what you must have meant as a month since
 I walk'd,

As I walk'd in silence the transparent shadowy night,

As I saw you had something to tell as you bent to me night
 after night,

As you droop'd from the sky low down as if to my side,
 (while the other stars all look'd on,)

As we wander'd together the solemn night, (for something
 I know not what kept me from sleep,)

As the night advanced, and I saw on the rim of the west
 how full you were of woe,

As I stood on the rising ground in the breeze in the cool
 transparent night,

As I watch'd where you pass'd and was lost in the netherward
 black of the night,

As my soul in its trouble dissatisfied sank, as where you sad orb,

Concluded, dropt in the night, and was gone.


**9**

Sing on there in the swamp,

O singer bashful and tender, I hear your notes, I hear your call,

I hear, I come presently, I understand you,

But a moment I linger, for the lustrous star has detain'd me,

The star my departing comrade holds and detains me.


**10**

O how shall I warble myself for the dead one there I loved?

And how shall I deck my song for the large sweet soul that
 has gone?

And what shall my perfume be for the grave of him I love?

Sea-winds blown from east and west,
Blown from the Eastern sea and blown from the Western
  sea, till there on the prairies meeting,
These and with these and the breath of my chant,
I'll perfume the grave of him I love.


**11**

O what shall I hang on the chamber walls?
And what shall the pictures be that I hang on the walls,
To adorn the burial-house of him I love?


Pictures of growing spring and farms and homes,
With the Fourth-month eve at sundown, and the gray smoke
  lucid and bright,
With floods of the yellow gold of the gorgeous, indolent,
  sinking sun, burning, expanding the air,
With the fresh sweet herbage under foot, and the pale green
  leaves of the trees prolific,
In the distance the flowing glaze, the breast of the river,
  with a wind-dapple here and there,
With ranging hills on the banks, with many a line against
  the sky, and shadows,
And the city at hand with dwellings so dense, and stacks of
  chimneys,
And all the scenes of life and the workshops, and the
  workmen homeward returning.


**12**

Lo, body and soul—this land,
My own Manhattan with spires, and the sparkling and
  hurrying tides, and the ships,

The varied and ample land, the South and the North in the
   light, Ohio's shores and flashing Missouri,
And ever the far-spreading prairies cover'd with grass and
   corn.

Lo, the most excellent sun so calm and haughty,
The violet and purple morn with just-felt breezes,
The gentle soft-born measureless light,
The miracle spreading bathing all, the fulfill'd noon,
The coming eve delicious, the welcome night and the stars,
Over my cities shining all, enveloping man and land.

## 13

Sing on, sing on you gray-brown bird,
Sing from the swamps, the recesses, pour your chant from
   the bushes,
Limitless out of the dusk, out of the cedars and pines.

Sing on dearest brother, warble your reedy song,
Loud human song, with voice of uttermost woe.

O liquid and free and tender!
O wild and loose to my soul—O wondrous singer!
You only I hear—yet the star holds me, (but will soon
   depart,)
Yet the lilac with mastering odor holds me.

## 14

Now while I sat in the day and look'd forth,
In the close of the day with its light and the fields of spring,
   and the farmers preparing their crops,

In the large unconscious scenery of my land with its lakes
and forests,
In the heavenly aerial beauty, (after the perturb'd winds and
the storms,)
Under the arching heavens of the afternoon swift passing,
and the voices of children and women,
The many-moving sea-tides, and I saw the ships how they
sail'd,
And the summer approaching with richness, and the fields
all busy with labor,
And the infinite separate houses, how they all went on, each
with its meals and minutia of daily usages,
And the streets how their throbbings throbb'd, and the cities
pent—lo, then and there,
Falling upon them all and among them all, enveloping me
with the rest,
Appear'd the cloud, appear'd the long black trail,
And I knew death, its thought, and the sacred knowledge
of death.

Then with the knowledge of death as walking one side of
me,
And the thought of death close-walking the other side of
me,
And I in the middle as with companions, and as holding
the hands of companions,
I fled forth to the hiding receiving night that talks not,
Down to the shores of the water, the path by the swamp in
the dimness,
To the solemn shadowy cedars and ghostly pines so still.

And the singer so shy to the rest receiv'd me,

The gray-brown bird I know receiv'd us comrades three,
And he sang the carol of death, and a verse for him I love.

From deep secluded recesses,
From the fragrant cedars and the ghostly pines so still,
Came the carol of the bird.

And the charm of the carol rapt me,
As I held as if by their hands my comrades in the night,
And the voice of my spirit tallied the song of the bird.

Come lovely and soothing death,
Undulate round the world, serenely arriving, arriving,
In the day, in the night, to all, to each,
Sooner or later delicate death.

Prais'd be the fathomless universe,
For life and joy, and for objects and knowledge curious,
And for love, sweet love—but praise! praise! praise!
For the sure-enwinding arms of cool-enfolding death.

Dark mother always gliding near with soft feet,
Have none chanted for thee a chant of fullest welcome?
Then I chant it for thee, I glorify thee above all,
I bring thee a song that when thou must indeed come, come
    unfalteringly.

Approach strong deliveress,
When it is so, when thou hast taken them I joyously sing
    the dead,
Lost in the loving floating ocean of thee,
Laved in the flood of thy bliss O death.

From me to thee glad serenades,
Dances for thee I propose saluting thee, adornments and
  feastings for thee,
And the sights of the open landscape and the high-spread
  sky are fitting,
And life and the fields, and the huge and thoughtful night.

The night in silence under many a star,
The ocean shore and the husky whispering wave whose
  voice I know,
And the soul turning to thee O vast and well-veil'd death,
And the body gratefully nestling close to thee.

Over the tree-tops I float thee a song,
Over the rising and sinking waves, over the myriad fields
  and the prairies wide,
Over the dense-pack'd cities all and the teeming wharves
  and ways,
I float this carol with joy, with joy to thee O death.

## 15
To the tally of my soul,
Loud and strong kept up the gray-brown bird,
With pure deliberate notes spreading filling the night.

Loud in the pines and cedars dim,
Clear in the freshness moist and the swamp-perfume,
And I with my comrades there in the night.

While my sight that was bound in my eyes unclosed,
As to long panoramas of visions.

And I saw askant the armies,

I saw as in noiseless dreams hundreds of battle-flags,

Borne through the smoke of the battles and pierc'd with
missiles I saw them,

And carried hither and yon through the smoke, and torn
and bloody,

And at last but a few shreds left on the staffs, (and all in
silence,)

And the staffs all splinter'd and broken.

I saw battle-corpses, myriads of them,

And the white skeletons of young men, I saw them,

I saw the debris and debris of all the slain soldiers of the
war,

But I saw they were not as was thought,

They themselves were fully at rest, they suffer'd not,

The living remain'd and suffer'd, the mother suffer'd,

And the wife and the child and the musing comrade suffer'd,

And the armies that remain'd suffer'd.

## 16

Passing the visions, passing the night,

Passing, unloosing the hold of my comrades' hands,

Passing the song of the hermit bird and the tallying song
of my soul,

Victorious song, death's outlet song, yet varying ever-altering
song,

As low and wailing, yet clear the notes, rising and falling,
flooding the night,

Sadly sinking and fainting, as warning and warning, and yet
again bursting with joy,

Covering the earth and filling the spread of the heaven,

As that powerful psalm in the night I heard from recesses,
Passing, I leave thee lilac with heart-shaped leaves,
I leave thee there in the door-yard, blooming, returning with
   spring.


I cease from my song for thee,
From my gaze on thee in the west, fronting the west,
   communing with thee,
O comrade lustrous with silver face in the night.


Yet each to keep and all, retrievements out of the night,
The song, the wondrous chant of the gray-brown bird,
And the tallying chant, the echo arous'd in my soul,
With the lustrous and drooping star with the countenance
   full of woe,
With the holders holding my hand nearing the call of the
   bird,
Comrades mine and I in the midst, and their memory ever
   to keep, for the dead I loved so well,
For the sweetest, wisest soul of all my days and lands—and
   this for his dear sake,
Lilac and star and bird twined with the chant of my soul,
There in the fragrant pines and the cedars dusk and dim.

# O Captain! My Captain!

O Captain! my Captain! our fearful trip is done,
The ship has weather'd every rack, the prize we sought is
    won,
The port is near, the bells I hear, the people all exulting,
While follow eyes the steady keel, the vessel grim and daring;
    But O heart! heart! heart!
      O the bleeding drops of red,
        Where on the deck my Captain lies,
          Fallen cold and dead.

O Captain! my Captain! rise up and hear the bells;
Rise up—for you the flag is flung—for you the bugle trills,
For you bouquets and ribbon'd wreaths—for you the shores
    a-crowding,
For you they call, the swaying mass, their eager faces turning;
    Here Captain! dear father!
      This arm beneath your head!
        It is some dream that on the deck,
          You've fallen cold and dead.

My Captain does not answer, his lips are pale and still,
My father does not feel my arm, he has no pulse nor will,
The ship is anchor'd safe and sound, its voyage closed and
    done,
From fearful trip the victor ship comes in with object won;
    Exult O shores, and ring O bells!
      But I with mournful tread,
        Walk the deck my Captain lies,
          Fallen cold and dead.

## One's-Self I Sing

One's-self I sing, a simple separate person,
Yet utter the word Democratic, the word En-Masse.

Of physiology from top to toe I sing,
Not physiognomy alone nor brain alone is worthy for the
   Muse, I say the Form complete is worthier far,
The Female equally with the Male I sing.

Of Life immense in passion, pulse, and power,
Cheerful, for freest action form'd under the laws divine,
The Modern Man I sing.

## As If A Phantom Caress'd Me

As if a phantom caress'd me,
I thought I was not alone walking here by the shore;
But the one I thought was with me as now I walk by the shore,
  the one I loved that caress'd me,
As I lean and look through the glimmering light—that one has
  utterly disappear'd,
And those appear that are hateful to me and mock me.

# In Cabin'd Ships At Sea

In cabin'd ships at sea,
The boundless blue on every side expanding,
With whistling winds and music of the waves, the large
imperious waves,
Or some lone bark buoy'd on the dense marine,
Where joyous full of faith, spreading white sails,
She cleaves the ether mid the sparkle and the foam of day,
or under many a star at night,
By sailors young and old haply will I, a reminiscence of the
land, be read,
In full rapport at last.

*Here are our thoughts, voyagers' thoughts,*
*Here not the land, firm land, alone appears, may then by them be*
*said,*
*The sky o'erarches here, we feel the undulating deck beneath our feet,*
*We feel the long pulsation, ebb and flow of endless motion,*
*The tones of unseen mystery, the vague and vast suggestions of the briny*
*world, the liquid-flowing syllables,*
*The perfume, the faint creaking of the cordage, the melancholy rhythm,*
*The boundless vista and the horizon far and dim are all here,*
*And this is ocean's poem.*

Then falter not O book, fulfil your destiny,
You not a reminiscence of the land alone,
You too as a lone bark cleaving the ether, purpos'd I know
not whither, yet ever full of faith,
Consort to every ship that sails, sail you!
Bear forth to them folded my love, (dear mariners, for you
I fold it here in every leaf;)

Speed on my book! spread your white sails my little bark
   athwart the imperious waves,
Chant on, sail on, bear o'er the boundless blue from me to
   every sea,
This song for mariners and all their ships.

## To You

Whoever you are, I fear you are walking the walks of dreams,
I fear these supposed realities are to melt from under your
    feet and hands,
Even now your features, joys, speech, house, trade,
    manners, troubles, follies, costume, crimes, dissipate away
    from you,
Your true soul and body appear before me,
They stand forth out of affairs, out of commerce, shops, work,
    farms, clothes, the house, buying, selling, eating, drinking,
    suffering, dying.

Whoever you are, now I place my hand upon you, that you
    be my poem,
I whisper with my lips close to your ear,
I have loved many women and men, but I love none better
    than you.

O I have been dilatory and dumb,
I should have made my way straight to you long ago,
I should have blabb'd nothing but you, I should have chanted
    nothing but you.

I will leave all and come and make the hymns of you,
None has understood you, but I understand you,
None has done justice to you, you have not done justice to
    yourself,
None but has found you imperfect, I only find no imper-
    fection in you,
None but would subordinate you, I only am he who will
    never consent to subordinate you,

I only am he who places over you no master, owner, better,
   God, beyond what waits intrinsically in yourself.

Painters have painted their swarming groups and the centre-
   figure of all,
From the head of the centre-figure spreading a nimbus of
   gold-color'd light,
But I paint myriads of heads, but paint no head without its
   nimbus of gold-color'd light,
From my hand from the brain of every man and woman it
   streams, effulgently flowing forever.

O I could sing such grandeurs and glories about you!
You have not known what you are, you have slumber'd upon
   yourself all your life,
Your eyelids have been the same as closed most of the time,
What you have done returns already in mockeries,
(Your thrift, knowledge, prayers, if they do not return in
   mockeries, what is their return?)

The mockeries are not you,
Underneath them and within them I see you lurk,
I pursue you where none else has pursued you,
Silence, the desk, the flippant expression, the night, the
   accustom'd routine, if these conceal you from others or
   from yourself, they do not conceal you from me,
The shaved face, the unsteady eye, the impure complexion,
   if these balk others they do not balk me,
The pert apparel, the deform'd attitude, drunkenness, greed,
   premature death, all these I part aside.

There is no endowment in man or woman that is not tallied
in you,
There is no virtue, no beauty in man or woman, but as
good is in you,
No pluck, no endurance in others, but as good is in you,
No pleasure waiting for others, but an equal pleasure waits
for you.

As for me, I give nothing to any one except I give the like
carefully to you,
I sing the songs of the glory of none, not God, sooner than
I sing the songs of the glory of you.

Whoever you are! claim your own at any hazard!
These shows of the East and West are tame compared to
you,
These immense meadows, these interminable rivers, you are
immense and interminable as they,
These furies, elements, storms, motions of Nature, throes of
apparent dissolution, you are he or she who is master or
mistress over them,
Master or mistress in your own right over Nature, elements,
pain, passion, dissolution.

The hopples fall from your ankles, you find an unfailing
sufficiency,
Old or young, male or female, rude, low, rejected by the
rest, whatever you are promulges itself,
Through birth, life, death, burial, the means are provided,
nothing is scanted,
Through angers, losses, ambition, ignorance, ennui, what
you are picks its way.

## I Dream'd In A Dream

I dream'd in a dream I saw a city invincible to the attacks
   of the whole of the rest of the earth,
I dream'd that was the new city of Friends,
Nothing was greater there than the quality of robust love—
   it led the rest,
It was seen every hour in the actions of the men of that
   city,
And in all their looks and words.

## That Shadow My Likeness

That shadow my likeness that goes to and fro seeking a
    livelihood, chattering, chaffering,
How often I find myself standing and looking at it where
    it flits,
How often I question and doubt whether that is really me;
But among my lovers and caroling these songs,
O I never doubt whether that is really me.

## We Two Boys Together Clinging

We two boys together clinging,
One the other never leaving,
Up and down the roads going, North and South excursions
  making,
Power enjoying, elbows stretching, fingers clutching,
Arm'd and fearless, eating, drinking, sleeping, loving,
No law less than ourselves owning, sailing, soldiering,
  thieving, threatening,
Misers, menials, priests alarming, air breathing, water
  drinking, on the turf or the sea-beach dancing,
Cities wrenching, ease scorning, statutes mocking, feebleness
  chasing,
Fulfilling our foray.

# Of Him I Love Day And Night

Of him I love day and night I dream'd I heard he was dead,
And I dream'd I went where they had buried him I love—
    but he was not in that place,
And I dream'd I wander'd searching among burial-places to
    find him,
And I found that every place was a burial-place;
The houses full of life were equally full of death, (this house
    is now,)
The streets, the shipping, the places of amusement, the
    Chicago, Boston, Philadelphia, the Mannahatta, were as full
    of the dead as of the living,
And fuller, O vastly fuller of the dead than of the living;
—And what I dream'd I will henceforth tell to every person
    and age,
And I stand henceforth bound to what I dream'd,
And now I am willing to disregard burial-places and dispense
    with them,
And if the memorials of the dead were put up indifferently
    everywhere, even in the room where I eat or sleep, I should
    be satisfied,
And if the corpse of any one I love, or if my own corpse,
    be duly render'd to powder and pour'd in the sea, I shall
    be satisfied,
Or if it be distributed to the winds I shall be satisfied.

## A Glimpse

A glimpse through an interstice caught,
Of a crowd of workmen and drivers in a bar-room around
    the stove late of a winter night, and I unremark'd seated
    in a corner,
Of a youth who loves me and whom I love, silently
    approaching and seating himself near, that he may hold
    me by the hand,
A long while amid the noises of coming and going, of
    drinking and oath and smutty jest,
There we two, content, happy in being together, speaking
    little, perhaps not a word.

## Are You The New Person Drawn Toward Me?

Are you the new person drawn toward me?
To begin with take warning—I am surely far different from
  what you suppose;
Do you suppose you will find in me your ideal?
Do you think it so easy to have me become your lover?
Do you think the friendship of me would be unalloy'd
  satisfaction?
Do you think I am trusty and faithful?
Do you see no further than this façade—this smooth and
  tolerant manner of me?
Do you suppose yourself advancing on real ground toward
  a real heroic man?
Have you no thought O dreamer that it may be all maya,
  illusion?

## To A Stranger

Passing stranger! you do not know how longingly I look
upon you,
You must be he I was seeking, or she I was seeking, (it
comes to me as of a dream,)
I have somewhere surely lived a life of joy with you,
All is recall'd as we flit by each other, fluid, affectionate,
chaste, matured,
You grew up with me, were a boy with me or a girl with
me,
I ate with you and slept with you—your body has become
not yours only nor left my body mine only,
You give me the pleasure of your eyes, face, flesh, as we
pass—you take of my beard, breast, hands, in return,
I am not to speak to you—I am to think of you when I sit
alone or wake at night alone,
I am to wait—I do not doubt I am to meet you again,
I am to see to it that I do not lose you.

## Sometimes With One I Love

Sometimes with one I love, I fill myself with rage, for fear I
 effuse unreturn'd love;
But now I think there is no unreturn›d love—the pay is certain,
 one way or another;
(I loved a certain person ardently, and my love was not return'd;
Yet out of that, I have written these songs.)

## A Leaf For Hand In Hand

A leaf for hand in hand;
You natural persons old and young!
You on the Mississippi and on all the branches and bayous
    of the Mississippi!
You friendly boatmen and mechanics! you roughs!
You twain! and all processions moving along the streets!
I wish to infuse myself among you till I see it common for
    you to walk hand in hand.

## Earth, My Likeness

Earth, my likeness,
Though you look so impassive, ample and spheric there,
I now suspect that is not all;
I now suspect there is something fierce in you eligible to
  burst forth,
For an athlete is enamour'd of me, and I of him,
But toward him there is something fierce and terrible in me
  eligible to burst forth,
I dare not tell it in words, not even in these songs.

## Fast Anchor'd, Eternal, O Love!

Fast anchor'd, eternal, O love! O woman I love!
O bride! O wife! more resistless than I can tell, the thought
  of you!
Then separate, as disembodied or another born,
Ethereal, the last athletic reality, my consolation,
I ascend, I float in the regions of your love O man,
O sharer of my roving life.

## Once I Pass'd Through A Populous City

Once I pass'd through a populous city imprinting my brain
    for future use with its shows, architecture, customs, tradi-
    tions,
Yet now of all that city I remember only a woman I casually
    met there who detain'd me for love of me,
Day by day and night by night we were together—all else
    has long been forgotten by me,
I remember I say only that woman who passionately clung
    to me,
Again we wander, we love, we separate again,
Again she holds me by the hand, I must not go,
I see her close beside me with silent lips sad and tremulous.

## A Noiseless Patient Spider

A noiseless patient spider,
I mark'd where on a little promontory it stood isolated,
Mark'd how to explore the vacant vast surrounding,
It launch'd forth filament, filament, filament, out of itself,
Ever unreeling them, ever tirelessly speeding them.

And you O my soul where you stand,
Surrounded, detached, in measureless oceans of space,
Ceaselessly musing, venturing, throwing, seeking the spheres
   to connect them,
Till the bridge you will need be form'd, till the ductile
   anchor hold,
Till the gossamer thread you fling catch somewhere, O my
   soul.

## This Dust Was Once The Man

This dust was once the man,
Gentle, plain, just and resolute, under whose cautious hand,
Against the foulest crime in history known in any land or
   age,
Was saved the Union of these States.

# I Sit And Look Out

I sit and look out upon all the sorrows of the world, and
  upon all oppression and shame,
I hear secret convulsive sobs from young men at anguish
  with themselves, remorseful after deeds done,
I see in low life the mother misused by her children, dying,
  neglected, gaunt, desperate,
I see the wife misused by her husband, I see the treacherous
  seducer of young women,
I mark the ranklings of jealousy and unrequited love
  attempted to be hid, I see these sights on the earth,
I see the workings of battle, pestilence, tyranny, I see martyrs
  and prisoners,
I observe a famine at sea, I observe the sailors casting lots
  who shall be kill'd to preserve the lives of the rest,
I observe the slights and degradations cast by arrogant
  persons upon laborers, the poor, and upon negroes, and
  the like;
All these—all the meanness and agony without end I sitting
  look out upon,
See, hear, and am silent.

## Year Of Meteors
(1859–60.)

Year of meteors! brooding year!
I would bind in words retrospective some of your deeds
  and signs,
I would sing your contest for the 19th Presidentiad,
I would sing how an old man, tall, with white hair, mounted
  the scaffold in Virginia,
(I was at hand—silent I stood with teeth shut close, I watch'd,
I stood very near you old man when cool and indifferent,
  but trembling with age and your unheal'd wounds you
  mounted the scaffold;)
I would sing in my copious song your census returns of the
  States,
The tables of population and products—I would sing of
  your ships and their cargoes,
The proud black ships of Manhattan arriving, some fill'd
  with immigrants, some from the isthmus with cargoes of
  gold,
Songs thereof would I sing—to all that hitherward comes
  would I welcome give,
And you would I sing, fair stripling! welcome to you from
  me, young prince of England!
Remember you surging Manhattan's crowds as you pass'd
  with your cortege of nobles?
There in the crowds stood I, and singled you out with
  attachment;
I know not why, but I loved you . . . (so go forth little
  song,
Far over sea speed like an arrow, carrying my love all folded,

And find in his palace the youth I love, and drop these lines
at my feet;)
Nor forget I to sing of the wonder, the ship as she swam
up my bay,
Well-shaped and stately the Great Eastern swam up my bay,
she was 600 feet long,
Her moving swiftly surrounded by myriads of small craft I
forget not to sing;
Nor the comet that came unannounced out of the north
flaring in heaven,
Nor the strange huge meteor-procession dazzling and clear
shooting over our heads,
(A moment, a moment long it sail'd its balls of unearthly
light over our heads,
Then departed, dropt in the night, and was gone;)
—Of such, and fitful as they, I sing—with gleams from them
would I gleam and patch these chants,
Your chants, O year all mottled with evil and good—year
of forebodings!
Year of comets and meteors transient and strange—lo! even
here one equally transient and strange!
As I flit through you hastily, soon to fall and be gone, what
is this chant,
What am I myself but one of your meteors?

## On The Beach At Night.

On the beach at night,
Stands a child with her father,
Watching the east, the autumn sky.

Up through the darkness,
While ravening clouds, the burial clouds, in black masses
  spreading,
Lower sullen and fast athwart and down the sky,
Amid a transparent clear belt of ether yet left in the east,
Ascends large and calm the lord-star Jupiter,
And nigh at hand, only a very little above,
Swim the delicate sisters the Pleiades.

From the beach the child holding the hand of her father,
Those burial-clouds that lower victorious soon to devour
  all,
Watching, silently weeps.

Weep not, child,
Weep not, my darling,
With these kisses let me remove your tears,
The ravening clouds shall not long be victorious,
They shall not long possess the sky, they devour the stars
  only in apparition,
Jupiter shall emerge, be patient, watch again another night,
  the Pleiades shall emerge,
They are immortal, all those stars both silvery and golden
  shall shine out again,
The great stars and the little ones shall shine out again, they
  endure,

The vast immortal suns and the long-enduring pensive
  moons shall again shine.

Then dearest child mournest thou only for Jupiter?
Considerest thou alone the burial of the stars?

Something there is,
(With my lips soothing thee, adding I whisper,
I give thee the first suggestion, the problem and indirection,)
Something there is more immortal even than the stars,
(Many the burials, many the days and nights, passing away,)
Something that shall endure longer even than lustrous Jupiter,
Longer than sun or any revolving satellite,
Or the radiant sisters the Pleiades.

# Whispers of Heavenly Death

Whispers of heavenly death murmur'd I hear,
Labial gossip of night, sibilant chorals,
Footsteps gently ascending, mystical breezes wafted soft and
    low,
Ripples of unseen rivers, tides of a current flowing, forever
    flowing,
(Or is it the plashing of tears? the measureless waters of
    human tears?)

I see, just see skyward, great cloud-masses,
Mournfully slowly they roll, silently swelling and mixing,
With at times a half-dimm'd sadden'd far-off star,
Appearing and disappearing.

(Some parturition rather, some solemn immortal birth;
On the frontiers to eyes impenetrable,
Some soul is passing over.)

## Hush'd Be The Camps To-Day
(May 4, 1865.)

Hush'd be the camps to-day,
And soldiers let us drape our war-worn weapons,
And each with musing soul retire to celebrate,
Our dear commander's death.

No more for him life's stormy conflicts,
Nor victory, nor defeat—no more time's dark events,
Charging like ceaseless clouds across the sky.

But sing poet in our name,
Sing of the love we bore him—because you, dweller in
  camps, know it truly.

As they invault the coffin there,
Sing—as they close the doors of earth upon him—one verse,
For the heavy hearts of soldiers.

## For You O Democracy

Come, I will make the continent indissoluble,
I will make the most splendid race the sun ever shone upon,
I will make divine magnetic lands,
  With the love of comrades,
  With the life-long love of comrades.

I will plant companionship thick as trees along all the rivers
  of America, and along the shores of the great lakes, and
  all over the prairies,
I will make inseparable cities with their arms about each
  other's necks,
  By the love of comrades,
  By the manly love of comrades.

For you these from me, O Democracy, to serve you ma
  femme!
For you, for you I am trilling these songs.

## As The Time Draws Nigh

As the time draws nigh glooming a cloud,
A dread beyond of I know not what darkens me.

I shall go forth,
I shall traverse the States awhile—but I cannot tell whither
  or how long,
Perhaps soon some day or night while I am singing my
  voice will suddenly cease.

O book, O chants! must all then amount to but this?
Must we barely arrive at this beginning of us? . . . and yet
  it is enough, O soul;
O soul, we have positively appear'd—that is enough.

## The Dalliance Of The Eagles

Skirting the river road, (my forenoon walk, my rest,)
Skyward in air a sudden muffled sound, the dalliance of the
  eagles,
The rushing amorous contact high in space together,
The clinching interlocking claws—a living, fierce, gyrating
  wheel,
Four beating wings—two beaks—a swirling mass tight
  grappling,
In tumbling turning clustering loops, straight downward
  falling,
Till o'er the river pois'd, the twain yet one, a moment's lull,
A motionless still balance in the air—then parting, talons
  loosing,
Upward again on slow-firm pinions slanting, their separate
  diverse flight,
She hers, he his, pursuing.

# America

Centre of equal daughters, equal sons,
All, all alike endear'd, grown, ungrown, young or old,
Strong, ample, fair, enduring, capable, rich,
Perennial with the Earth, with Freedom, Law and Love,
A grand, sane, towering, seated Mother,
Chair'd in the adamant of Time.

## Had I The Choice

Had I the choice to tally greatest bards,
To limn their portraits, stately, beautiful, and emulate at will,
Homer with all his wars and warriors—Hector, Achilles,
   Ajax,
Or Shakspere's woe-entangled Hamlet, Lear, Othello—
   Tennyson's fair ladies,
Metre or wit the best, or choice conceit to wield in perfect
   rhyme, delight of singers;
These, these, O sea, all these I'd gladly barter,
Would you the undulation of one wave, its trick to me
   transfer,
Or breathe one breath of yours upon my verse,
And leave its odor there.

# O Me! O Life!

O me! O life! of the questions of these recurring,
Of the endless trains of the faithless, of cities fill'd with the
   foolish,
Of myself forever reproaching myself, (for who more foolish
   than I, and who more faithless?)
Of eyes that vainly crave the light, of the objects mean, of
   the struggle ever renew'd,
Of the poor results of all, of the plodding and sordid crowds
   I see around me,
Of the empty and useless years of the rest, with the rest me
   intertwined,
The question, O me! so sad, recurring—What good amid
   these,
O me, O life?

*Answer.*
That you are here—that life exists and identity,
That the powerful play goes on, and you may contribute a
   verse.

## Prayer Of Columbus

A batter'd, wreck'd old man,
Thrown on this savage shore, far, far from home,
Pent by the sea and dark rebellious brows, twelve dreary
  months,
Sore, stiff with many toils, sicken'd and nigh to death,
I take my way along the island's edge,
Venting a heavy heart.

I am too full of woe!
Hapl y I may not live another day;
I cannot rest O God, I cannot eat or drink or sleep,
Till I put forth myself, my prayer, once more to Thee,
Breathe, bathe myself once more in Thee, commune with
  Thee,
Report myself once more to Thee.

Thou knowest my years entire, my life,
My long and crowded life of active work, not adoration
  merely;
Thou knowest the prayers and vigils of my youth,
Thou knowest my manhood's solemn and visionary medi-
  tations,
Thou knowest how before I commenced I devoted all to
  come to Thee,
Thou knowest I have in age ratified all those vows and strictly
  kept them,
Thou knowest I have not once lost nor faith nor ecstasy in
  Thee,
In shackles, prison'd, in disgrace, repining not,
Accepting all from Thee, as duly come from Thee.

All my emprises have been fill'd with Thee,

My speculations, plans, begun and carried on in thoughts
of Thee,

Sailing the deep or journeying the land for Thee;

Intentions, purports, aspirations mine, leaving results to Thee.


O I am sure they really came from Thee,

The urge, the ardor, the unconquerable will,

The potent, felt, interior command, stronger than words,

A message from the Heavens whispering to me even in sleep,

These sped me on.


By me and these the work so far accomplish'd,

By me earth's elder cloy'd and stifled lands uncloy'd, unloos'd,

By me the hemispheres rounded and tied, the unknown to
the known.


The end I know not, it is all in Thee,

Or small or great I know not—haply what broad fields, what
lands,

Haply the brutish measureless human undergrowth I know,

Transplanted there may rise to stature, knowledge worthy
Thee,

Haply the swords I know may there indeed be turn'd to
reaping-tools,

Haply the lifeless cross I know, Europe's dead cross, may
bud and blossom there.


One effort more, my altar this bleak sand;

That Thou O God my life hast lighted,

With ray of light, steady, ineffable, vouchsafed of Thee,

Light rare untellable, lighting the very light,

Beyond all signs, descriptions, languages;
For that O God, be it my latest word, here on my knees,
Old, poor, and paralyzed, I thank Thee.

My terminus near,
The clouds already closing in upon me,
The voyage balk'd, the course disputed, lost,
I yield my ships to Thee.

My hands, my limbs grow nerveless,
My brain feels rack'd, bewilder'd,
Let the old timbers part, I will not part,
I will cling fast to Thee, O God, though the waves buffet
    me,
Thee, Thee at least I know.

Is it the prophet's thought I speak, or am I raving?
What do I know of life? what of myself?
I know not even my own work past or present,
Dim ever-shifting guesses of it spread before me,
Of newer better worlds, their mighty parturition,
Mocking, perplexing me.

And these things I see suddenly, what mean they?
As if some miracle, some hand divine unseal'd my eyes,
Shadowy vast shapes smile through the air and sky,
And on the distant waves sail countless ships,
And anthems in new tongues I hear saluting me.

# Index of First Lines